TONY
BENNETT

Also by Tony Jasper

BARRY MANILOW
JOHNNY: The Authorised Biography of Johnny Mathis

TONY BENNETT

A biography by
Tony Jasper

W.H. ALLEN · LONDON

COMET

Typeset by Phoenix Photosetting
Printed and bound in Great Britain by
Mackays of Chatham Ltd, Kent
for the Publishers, W.H. Allen & Co. PLC
44 Hill Street, London W1X 8LB

ISBN 0 491 03203 X (W.H. Allen hardcover edition)
ISBN 0 86379 008 9 (Comet Books softcover edition)

To the late and much respected music writer Dick Tatham

For Edward and May Bryson
Ronald and Joan Veltman

Author's Note

This study of Tony Bennett falls into three sections. The first is a careful examination of Bennett the man, his artistry, and an overall appreciation of his career. The second traces Tony through the four decades in which his career has blossomed. The third is a detailed discography and charting of his record successes.

My thanks to Pat Doncaster, Max Jones, Derek Witt, Rodney Burbeck, Ernie Anderson, Forbes Cameron and many other writers for their thoughts and recollections.

Contents

Introduction

TONY BENNETT IS one of the outstanding and unique vocalists of twentieth-century contemporary music and one of the great singers from the 1950s onwards. This is the story of the man and his music.

As Ernie Anderson, an American and long-time friend and associate of Bennett says: 'The guy is the same today as he was when he began thirty or more years ago. He didn't start out imitating anyone – he was just himself. He's always been TB! There is no-one like him who travels the world, who presents his concerts immaculately. He pays out for a first class orchestra and, even if audiences don't notice, he has chaperoned and introduced to a wider market some first-class musicians like Bobby Hackett or Ruby Braff. What he's doing tonight, tomorrow night, any night is what he's been doing for forty years. The guy sells out wherever he goes – he keeps selling the tickets. He's extraordinary. If no-one bothers about him then he goes out and gets the audience and he's the hottest ticket of the year. Time is always Bennett time: whatever else may be happening, he always is. My opinion of Bennett, my judgement of Tony runs to the highest praise.'

To discover the reason why Bennett is regarded so highly and affectionately is one of the persistent, underlying preoccupations of this book. Another theme is his survival in an ever-changing musical world, the early hopes and dreams of the young man slowly developing and crystallizing the consummate skill of the professional artist.

Bennett's musical life has not been an easy one for if he has always had talent he has not by any means been given constant and imaginative exposure and promotion. Often he has talked of the non-creative people around in show business and bewailed their apparent desire to seek out the lowest common musical denominator.

'There's no mystery in music,' he says and adds pointedly that 'if it's good, it will sell. Think how a creative music like jazz could be promoted, and should be promoted. A great jazz group gets booked into a club, or gets recorded, and who hears about it? Sure, Louis Armstrong was promoted, and should have been. But he wasn't before Joe Glaser got behind him. Yes, Ella Fitzgerald is a big star, and should be, too. But only the aficionados knew Ella until Normal Granz helped her build audiences. And Duke Ellington. Yes, but Duke wrote his music, led his band and promoted himself, as he had to. Not everyone can carry all that weight by himself. Who promoted Charlie Parker? Who ever built stories around Billie Holiday that didn't try to sensationalise the tragic side of her life instead of promoting her singing? The jazz critics and the jazz magazines. But I'll be talking about all-out promotion to try to reach *all* people, not just the jazz fans. Did Billie Holiday and Charlie Parker have to die in poverty? And what about Art Tatum? George Gershwin came to hear Tatum play the piano, and so I could continue.'

But although sensitivity is in short supply in some quarters, Bennett has never lost money for anyone – club owner, concert promoter or record company. 'I've been told, "Tony, you can't do that," or "Tony, you've got to do this." I've done just the opposite. And it always comes out right.'

So his story is of a man with great self-belief and with supreme dedication to his own talent. 'I've sometimes taken months before I'm satisfied with a song. I've looked over hundreds of songs and those I do select then I sing over and over again, three or four hours a day – not till the song feels right, but till *I* feel right. You've got to do what you feel is right. And "feel" is the key word there.'

But Bennett has not always done the right thing and this story is not just a cap-doffing exercise, however great the man. He has at times succumbed to irresistible pressure and sung something that was foisted upon him. Later though he has tried to redress the situation. 'I just apologise when people ask for some songs and I say I sang them because I ignored my own judgement.'

This musical journey shows how Tony Bennett has endeared himself to musicians first and foremost and how his catalogue of songs has been drawn largely from the great classic writers. 'I like all the usual composers – Gershwin, Porter, Richard Rodgers and Larry Hart, Arlen, Mercer and the rest. If someone nailed me down to one composer, I would probably choose Jimmy Van Heusen. Just look at all those wonderful songs he wrote for Crosby and Sinatra.'

Tony Bennett will have more to say in this book on composers and musicians including those two greats, Basie and Ellington. I also hope to convey Tony Bennett's power to communicate with his audience and their rapture at his vocal dexterity. Much of the material has been gathered from interviews over the years in a wide variety of journals, as well as from the personal interviews I have had with Bennett's fans and with music critics who have studied this man's artistry. To the many who have talked with me or whose work I have read I pay tribute and give thanks. Oddly this is the first major study on Bennett – the fullest previous account is an interesting section in Ken Barnes' *Sinatra and the Great*

*Song Stylists.** If there is one overriding impression that I hope will emerge from this study, it is simply that there is a thing called Bennett magic!

Tony Jasper
London, 1984

* London, Ian Allen, 1972.

PART ONE

1.

Foundations

SINCE HIS ARTISTIC beginnings at the end of the 1940s there have been numerous trends which have superficially affected Tony Bennett's standing in the music world. His reputation, his record sales and contracts, releases and engagements have all been subject to ever-recurring analyses as new music, new people and new assumptions have sought to establish their own authority.

Bennett came from a slow-moving musical world that accepted the 'live' performer and expected a degree of quality which is rarely achieved in current recording circles. The decades have come and gone, accompanied by numerous fads and fashions. Ever since Elvis Presley and the Beatles, evanescence has been a norm of the music world. There has been an insistence on locating the 'new', with too little effort from all quarters to establish durable 'careers'. Some of pop's frenetic activity has come from its money-orientated philosophy but also from rapid developments in technology. Recording techniques, studio controls and ever-expanding track machines have contributed to the demise of the type of artist who is signed by virtue of sheer vocal ability or a high profile in performance and presentation. Current recording techniques can transform the ordinary voice while sophisticated production can disguise vocal inability and 'image' may replace actual musical ability as a priority in a record company's thinking. But all this was foreign to the Bennett of the late 1940s. He knew and heard the dance bands and singers. Even then, though he came at the tail end of an era, he was in time to savour the tastes and smells of a fading world.

His world talked of sheet music, and records were not yet so important. It was stage appearances and the sales of music scores that brought in the revenue. The publisher was king-pin and together with the agent more or less controlled what might happen in the music business. But, as Chapter 5 will show, early in the development of Tony's career Tin Pan Alley was heading for its demise – but this did not happen quickly enough for Tony to be unaware of its presence.

Rock would knock the long-lasting 'sacred' kingdoms from their perch; the record would replace sheet music; and the public would increasingly demand to hear the 'voice' as it sounded on record. But at their outset these developments would have seemed like nonsense to the artists of another era.

Bennett knew from an early age that he would have to learn his vocal trade and that he would not last unless he became a skilled practitioner, whereas aspiring pop singers were often unable to sing properly and certainly could not read music. They could not communicate with a band, an orchestra or even a group, for someone else took care of that, and a new breed of music man arose to bridge the gap. But Bennett and his contemporaries could communicate with anyone.

So – not surprisingly – throughout his career Tony Bennett assumed a set of standards that were alien to those who were to emerge in the late 1950s and the following decades. This led him to attack consistently the pop world in general and many of its performers in particular. Just occasionally he would find a kind word to say or would single out an artist – a McCartney, even a

Bobby Rydell – for praise. And he would record – albeit in different form, theatrical in voice and instrumentation – a song such as the Beatles 'Eleanor Rigby' or Stevie Wonder's 'My Cherie Amour' with soaring strings and a touch of show-biz richness. Outside his own rather poppish beginnings and some early flights into the simply constructed pop songs which had immediate commercial and eventual pop potential – for instance the pulsating, pounding song 'I Am' – Bennett would remain a 'quality' purveyor of popular music.

His beginnings meant that he had to learn real vocal projection and the importance of presentation. He has often linked the two in his public pronouncements, for instance in this statement from one of his press relations brochures:

Any singer can cut a record but only a star can make it happen in a performance. Performance and presentation count for everything in transforming a song into a work of art and making a star out of a singer. A good performer has the ability to become a true artist if he really puts his heart into it. It's what some people today call 'soul'.

This sentiment has clear assumptions – some of which have already been outlined and belong in general show-business consciousness to the late 1940s and the early part of the following decade. Bennett took with him the musical values of previous decades when an artist respected quality in a writer, both lyrically and musically, and when he insisted that he would sing 'good' material and not be tempted to lower his standards because the money might be more readily forthcoming. Tony Bennett would do more, for he would surround himself with the best of musicians and, because of his background, he would sing with the best in any field of popular music – jazz especially.

Bennett's work with Woody Herman, Ellington, Buddy

Rich and Count Basie particularly would represent the efforts of one professional with others of a similar calibre: in contrast to later pop extravaganzas where a rock band or singer would have a musical backcloth supplied by a classical orchestra but with a rather strained marrying of effects. As Rich said in 1968:

'Sinatra is singing greater today than he ever did. He has a total hold on his public. Artistically, musically and audience-wise he is a tremendous entertainer. But Sinatra thinks that Tony Bennett is the best singer in the country today. Tony has a great jazz feeling – both in ballads and jump things. He makes tremendous emotional impact.'

He would become a singer's singer, winning much more respect from fellow-performers and musicians than he sometimes found from music critics and later with the public at large. He would mix with the jazz fraternity but, like Sinatra, he would often be ignored in jazz journals and encyclopaedias. Some jazz purists would argue that he was off-pitch at the top, but then it might be argued that influential jazz figures have had similar traits. But the jazz world has often had strange ground rules and reasons as to who can be admitted within its hallowed halls.

In early times there were those who thought of him as no more than an interesting artist who might – for good or bad – be led into the blandness of pop. So when he ran riot with Basie they were surprised and delighted, abandoning any thoughts that he was just another singer. Bennett revealed that he could swing fairly well: he could place the notes. Later he would state clearly and unequivocally that he had straightened out his 'patching' problem.

Bennett belonged to a world where an artist, rather than a vast entourage of minions, thought it right that he should say and believe what he sang. It was called 'musical integrity'. It sounds sadly antiquated, but it is heartening. And it would produce some interesting clashes over the years.

When Bennett was billed for London's Pigalle theatre-restaurant in April 1961 much of the London press found difficulty in understanding why he should be invited when he was not a hit recording artist. Writers explained that he had been before, in 1951, after winning seventeen popularity polls and an award as 'Best Male Vocalist' but had only been loved by critics, leaving the general public unmoved. They pointed out his 'Stranger In Paradise', a one-time UK chart-topper. In a more kindly tone British music paper readers were told Bennett was an album-singer, as though members of the 33 rpm club are an alien breed. However Britain's *Record Mirror* congratulated Pigalle owner Al Burnett on using his instinct, rather than the deceptive sales barometer, in booking Tony.

Ironically it was Tony's nose that interested rather than his amazing track record and the fact that in a much larger country with higher standards overall he was rated second to Sinatra. 'Considering his mass of vocal talent Tony Bennett is perhaps being over-modest when he remarks: "I don't want to be hired because of my nose. I have succeeded in spite of it." An odd remark perhaps. But it seems Mr Bennett has a complex about his nose. He considers it over large. Worse than this, he says, "It looks as if it has been stepped on by the Brigade of Guards. I am not a pretty boy and I know it."'

The media's preoccupation with his breathing passages and organ of smell can only be compared with the 1980s' obsession with Barry Manilow's nose.

Another illustration of Bennett's battle with the elements of time comes in an outburst he made to *Daily Mirror's* show-biz editor Pat Doncaster, later co-author of the top-ten hardback *Cliff*, that there should be a new kind of record chart. Bennett was told by Doncaster that the US chart of the week, late April 1965, was heavily British.

'Of course the Beatles caused that,' said Tony, 'the impact they made was so strong. I believe they will be a permanent factor – but I don't think the rest will be lasting. Sure they're good records for dancing . . . but temporary.' Bennett, warming to his theme, explained how the chart was unrepresentative in that it told of sales over a short period and not of accumulating purchases. 'Look at the people you rarely see in the top ten, like Sinatra and Belafonte. They sell all the time and I don't think the charts reflect the true position.' Bennett advocated a chart system that would reflect sales over a period rather than over one week. But at least Bennett showed that he was in touch with the present by proclaiming proudly, 'I've got my personal mission accomplished in London. I've got the Beatles' autographs.'

Bennett projected – and still does – the image of being a good guy and he certainly became an important guy as time marched on. Talk with musicians and arrangers, club-owners and promoters, publicists and writers and the message is the same – Bennett is one of the lads.

Many recall the relaxed, happy Tony Bennett during the televising of ITV's *Tony Bennett at the Talk of the Town* – his first-ever TV series anywhere – in spite of the fact that he had fifty-three LPs under his belt. When he was not singing he remained to listen, appreciate and applaud other artists like Sarah Vaughan or the rich-sounding orchestra of friend Robert Farnon. Most artists would have disappeared from the scene. He talks with anyone who 'knows' and if he has ordered for himself and received the best treatment, whether in hotel service or tour arrangements, then it has not resulted in a rather boring star-studded monster (and the music world does have a goodly collection of ogres filled with their own pomposity who get 'served' because in the end they provide the 'bread and butter' to many). Max Jones, the revered British jazz writer and critic, recalls many delightful meetings with Bennett, an artist who had time to talk and who conveyed his own enthusiasms about his work and even that of others.

Max Jones says: 'He has no side. I recall Tony as an excellent host, jazz was the main thrust of our conversation when we dined once at London's Royal Festival Hall, and he loved Italian food! I think he was obsessed with music, and painting has become a stronger interest as time has progressed. He was keen, I remember on one occasion, for me to interview the marvellous trumpeter Bobby Hackett. He said Bobby is here and why not talk with him and it happend again with Ruby Braff.'*

And indeed Bennett has been fulsome in his praise of all and sundry wherever he feels praise is due. Obviously those he has worked with through the years have attracted much praise but along the way the man has praised Britain's delightful Annie Ross and a saxophone player, Pete King, Bennett heard at Annie's Room. Annie – on one occasion among many – guested with Bennett during his forty-five-minute BBC TV *Show of the Week* on 5 April 1967. She duetted with Tony and sang one of his hits 'The Good Life'. The programme provided a foretaste of the concert tour he made with Count Basie and his Orchestra the following month.

In the field of songwriting Bennett would over the years ask for greater recognition for people like Joe McCarthy Jr, Lalo Schifrin and Cy Coleman whom he regarded as heirs to the greatness of men like Jerome Kern and Cole Porter.

And one occasion saw him fighting for the Duke and his

*'A trumpet man of delightful Swing trumpet and rightfully, as critic-writer Joachim Berendt has said "full of grace and charm in Swing and Dixieland".' *The Joachim Berendt Jazz Book*, Hart-Davis MacGibbon, London, 1976.

23

music. Tony had expressed his feelings that teenagers will listen to good music if given the chance and courted a little. 'I said to a management one day that they should break precedent and have a special matinee of Duke Ellington for teenagers. So they told me I was crazy, or something. It wouldn't work they said. And if those kids even bother to turn up, they'll be so untidy they won't even listen. Well, I convinced the management. At both places where this happened they did turn away business – better than my adult audiences in the evening.'

Except in the early days, Bennett has never been known as an artist with a large accompanying entourage ('once I travelled with six managers in dark suits') nor as someone who accepts that a large company of people should control his movements. More than most artists he has directed his own development and in so doing has earned general respect, though far greater admiration has come from a panoply of stars who have from time to time paid compliments going beyond mere politeness and have even enthused in the manner and spirit of fans. The compliments paid to Bennett by a variety of people will be covered later in this book, but at least in this opening section it is appropriate to mention one particular legendary figure, the late Judy Garland.

Judy, interviewed in a suite on the fourteenth floor of a New York hotel, said: 'I remember the first time I heard Tony sing on a record. I thought "that *sound*! He isn't copying *anyone*!" His sound get into your ear and into your heart. To me, he's so much more important than any instrumentalist, because he *says* something important. He sings and phrases lyrics that are completely Tony Bennett. He tells a story with his songs.'

Garland, speaking to an unnamed interviewer, extolled Tony's professionalism, his magnificent voice and vocal control and, extending her eulogy beyond show-biz, she commented: 'I think the world needs Tony Bennett as much as I need to hear him. I think he's the epitome of what entertainers are put on earth for. He was born to take people's troubles away, even for an hour. He loves doing it. He's a giver.'

Judy proceeded with a dissertation on the music business world and some of the less savoury aspects of business dealings but having summarized the blotches and bleedings she ended with her view of Tony the 'man' and Tony in terms of the entertainment business. 'Tony has none of the showbusiness toughness or hardness you come to expect. He's unable to be hard; he's vulnerable – but masculine. I've never seen him lose his temper, but I hope he does, now and then. He is Tony Bennett, and there isn't any resemblance to anyone else. There's just one, and everybody had better appreciate him. Nobody knows what makes Tony Bennett tick. I don't. But whatever it is, I like it. He doesn't ask for anything more than to give. He really does give his heart to an audience, and of course they give him their hearts in return. Tony Bennett is the finest male entertainer in the world today!'

High praise, indeed. And from such a marvellous singer even higher than the highest praise, especially as she was speaking at a time when high standards of musical skill were expected from artists. But this kind of analysis belongs to a world which seems far past or is at least fading, though there have been some valiant attempts to regain some of its momentum. Within general pop circles several young singers have revived some of the old standard songs and have themselves reflected a jazz influence in their work. They have suggested that 'standards' might be returning though much of what they have done has fallen to the readiness of the music media to categorize songs as representing some new fad rather than to open up for young people the realization that there is enormous musical wealth which they have been denied. The industry does of course market quality from time to time (unless it happens purely by chance). But artists like Bennett have been the main sufferers and this attitude on the part of record companies has forced such artists to restrict their work to admittedly well-paid night clubs. But the escape of the 'quality' artists like Bennett from the clutches of the large companies has been as much to do with artists' dismay at their treatment as it has with the desire to take the money and run to or from Las Vegas.

Bennett over the years has refused to compromise, to water down his art for the sake of immediate gain and, doubtless, instant oblivion – if the general practice of pop is operative – once the 'topical' record has ceased to interest. In a sense wilfully he has engaged in battle with the powers that be, yet rather than being regarded as 'foolish' his integrity and concern for standards are cause for respect.

The likes of Tony Bennett are rare and some would add that few are the stars of his ilk whose record of behaviour is so remarkably unblemished. Bennett does not hit the gossip columns with super-star ego-blowing sessions that leave behind wanton destruction of property nor does the man abuse his body with excesses. Bennett's appearances in the tittle-tattle of show-biz columnists have come either as a result of his interest in painting or because of the several 'loves' in his life (both his artistic skills and his marital dilemmas are discussed in a later chapter).

Outside his control – and that of any other artist – is fan reaction and there are those who have chased Bennett as any groupies of whatever musical idiom, whether pop or classical. What he has made for himself is a wide circle of friends and these come from every social strata. Max Jones says that Bennett the man knows his own mind and one of the most powerful impressions he had found in meeting the artist is the 'individualistic' trait, a character-istic that permeates his overall attitude to show-business and is most clearly displayed in his relentless search for perfection. 'He insists on high quality. I don't think he's found any problems with British musicians, UK bands.' This inner belief has enabled him to withstand those who would wish him to have more instant commercial appeal and as later chapters will show he has been able to survive even blasts of cold air from the record and television industries. Though of course, even the ravages of time and the fluctuating movements within the pop world have not been able to prevent him performing.

His movements in the 1960s are traced elsewhere but suffice it to say here that before the Beatles hit the big time in Britain during 1963 Bennett had already accomplished a 'Who's Who' of the leading Stateside supper clubs including New York's Copacabana, the Dunes Hotel, Las Vegas, the Latin Casino in New Jersey, the Deauville Hotels and Boston's Blinstrub's. In 1963 he presented shows at the Town and Country Brooklyn and New York's Freedomland, drawing record-breaking crowds at both entertainments. And at the time plans were made for appearances at the Frolics Club in Boston, New York's famed resort the Concord, Houston's Cork Club.and New York City's Copacabana.

But Bennett did not wish to see his artistry and music caught merely by a supper-club audience and it was on this point that he ran headlong against time and the record and media world's obsession with only giving to youth music performed by youth. Bennett did not see experience, craft and classical material as something that meant relegation upstairs into middle-aged and older territory.

Brilliant British pianist Alan Clare who has accompanied Bennett says he can find nothing adverse to say about him. 'Tony has forged ahead on his own whatever else is happening in the popular musical world. He is one of those pure professionals. And anyway he loved my chords and harmonies.' Indeed Clare's sensitivity of touch and particularly the way he plays ballads married well with the artist's style. Alan's wife says the two had a mutual respect for each other's craft and saw how they could both gain from working together. 'You can only speak as you find. They both liked each other. Alan and Spike Milligan have written "Alice in Wonderland" and Alan played it to Tony and he said he loved it. Tony Bennett is a great musician and a great person.'

Bennett may often have seemed to be out of step with the changing times, but over the years he has had many great moments and has collected countless admirers from all walks of life. It may well be true that a Bennett born ten or twenty years earlier than his actual birth date could have been a much heralded and remembered singer within the great dance band era but speculation should not hide the man's essential greatness through decades where the hit record has been the main inspiration guiding television schedules, monetary expenditure and public adulation. Bennett offers comfort to any aspiring singer who feels the modern musical world offers scant reward for talent.

Towards the end of the 1970s the Columbia Records President of the day, Clive Davis (one of the most successful and inventive of all record company executives) told a UNLY audience that Bennett's big mistake was with his refusal to sing *commercial* material. But Bennett can lay claim to survival while some instant 'commercial' artist may now doubtless be found at a gas station in some obscure US town in the mid-West. Discriminating record buyers will always remain and will buy the records of the quality artist who has been able to withstand the cold sullen silence of record corporations obsessed with *Billboard*'s Hot 100 or, in the UK, *Music Week*'s Top 75. As Max Jones says: 'You just can't imagine anything Tony does to be in the least "bad taste" – his whole career has been built on class,' and to do so in an ever-changing musical world can only call for unqualified admiration.

2.

The Artist

TONY BENNETT WAS a kid who wanted to sing. And it is not surprising that his wish should have been granted. Certain artists are born to write songs. Bennett was placed on this earth to interpret them, to lift them off the page and make them something vital.

His career has been punctuated by a series of recurring 'highs' and coloured by frequent outbursts of enthusiasm from a master practitioner who has never tired of his art. Bennett, of the leather-lunged style of delivery on vocals in front of army bands and in small, sleezy nightclubs, became an all-time great who has frequently been called the 'singer's singer', an artist loved and respected by the humble and the mighty in the music business, from bandleaders and musicians to the people who serve the drinks or take the door money. CBS Corporate Publicity Manager Derek Witt recalls Bennett's amazing consideration one night in Oxford.

'Tony decided he wanted to give a supper party for the band. The question was where. The Chinese place was closed on a Sunday. So I went to the Randolph. I said, "What can you do?" I knew there was a nice restaurant there, a sort of steak house in the basement.

'I explained who it was for and who was giving it. I said there would be about sixty to seventy people. They said "Yes" so we got round to talking about basics. They said, "It's Sunday, no problem, we can do the food etcetera

31

and keep the staff on," but then they added "But no drink I'm afraid." So what do you do? I had a brainwave. I booked myself in, spent a night and had my own party and used room service! It was Tony's "do" of course. He was really pleased and so were the guys.'

Derek Witt says Bennett has always had a marvellous relationship with musicians. 'He's so kind and thoughtful. Once he trusts someone, fine. He'll say, "If Tony says so then it's OK, or Derek wants it, then fine." He's a great guy.'

Right from the beginning Bennett was known for his modesty and his reticence, and even when he had successes notched up in the form of gold discs he remained an unassuming artist. CBS executive Derek Witt recalls how the superstar volunteered to sing at the CBS manufacturing and distribution plant at Aylesbury.

'The staff have a Christmas "do" and we had on this occasion six to seven hundred people gathered at the Civic Hall, Dunstable. The policy of the family (CBS) is let them dance the night away later in the evening but first one of the CBS acts would entertain them.

'I remember we were stuck for someone. I thought I would stick my neck out and ask Tony. To my pleasure he said "fine" and the band, Bill Maynard's, with whom he was touring, agreed. The band got their MU rates and Tony and Bill did it for free. It was an incredible "do" – it was wonderful. A really kind and generous act.' He was from the outset, and has remained for the most part, uninterested in his publicity though at times he has been known to express anger at the treatment he may have received from the occasional errant journalist who, while writing about such an obviously talented artist, has for sure misunderstood or not bothered to assimilate the full power and impact of the singing act which has collected for Bennett the accolades of fellow artists.

He was known from the start as someone who was

willing to work at his art, who had an interest in vocalization beyond what might be the immediate return of a hit, and royalties and media attention. Bobby Hackett is one who remembers the early artist. 'We had a little jazz band in New York called The Hickory Log. Vic Dickinson was with us – who to me is the greatest trombone player in the world . . . And Ernie Caceres was in the band – I can't quite remember who else, it's quite a while ago.

'But this kid used to come in and want to sing with us. And we would let him come up and sing. And I knew immediately that he had it. And it was Tony Bennett.'

And if Bennett was not begging for the mike and stand then he was listening and doing the rounds of the clubs with an insatiable desire to hear and learn, to watch vocal technique and delivery and obtain a solid grounding which would stand him in good stead later in his career: 'I was able to hear some great music in those days – Billie Holiday, George Shearing, Art Tatum, Stan Getz, you name it.' It was a background that has often drawn despair from him when asked about the music which any aspiring artist of today might study. 'The music I hear today is very dissonant, very uneducated. It's simply not as mature as the music I grew up on. When I say that, I'm not just being sentimental. Nowadays I don't know what I'm listening to. Everything seems to be regressing into a sort of constant throbbing, a kind of cave-man music.'

Bennett names his exceptions – McCartney and Stevie Wonder are two – but as has been mentioned, in his early days before the cult of the teen pop star and the growth of studio, engineer and producer, there was the class singer-vocalist whose art was to interpret and implant their own skills to produce a fusion between artist-writer and accompaniment.

Tony's background and the riches around him subconsciously dictated to him that he would sing only tasteful music. This principle reached its peak expression when in the early 1970s his relations with US company Columbia (British CBS eventually) sunk to an all-time low. After several skirmishes and compromises he finally broke with them, announcing that he would not waste his career on recording drivel. 'Every artist has his dignity. When a record company says, "If you don't record this song, you'll lose your job," all they're doing is trying to frighten you into doing something you know you shouldn't be doing.'

But at the outset there was no need to make a choice and in any case he had to learn to trust his own judgement and gain from the best teacher of all – experience. In the early days Bennett learnt the ropes. He could find himself with all kinds of music: 'When I was with a dance band I had to sing everything in strict, square tempo.' Later, with success behind him, he could sing the numbers as he saw them. As he says: 'This song may be wrong to you as far as my treatment is concerned, but I can tell you that if I only feel it one way . . . then that's the *right* way for *me*.' But even limitations can be valuable and Bennett learnt much from the early restrictions. He learnt how to take something straight and how to adapt it until eventually a song becomes part and parcel of his own nature.

And in those early days when he was aspiring to be an artist of the highest calibre he was conscious of the high standard of songwriting in the 1930s, 1940s and early 1950s. 'There was great competition then. Gershwin, Cole Porter and Harold Arlen were all writing at the same time, and this helped the whole music business. Everybody was trying to write songs and write their songs better than the next and I really wish this would happen again.'

It was pianist Art Tatum who early on made a profound impression on Bennett and who gave him insights into how he might treat a song. 'He made every song a dramatic production. I couldn't copy his arpeggios. But his rubato, and his phrasing helped a lot. I met him once

34

when he was playing in Washington DC – that was when the racial thing was really bad, even in the shadow of the White House. They wouldn't let me into his dressing room. He had to come outside to say hello.'

And it was Louis Armstrong who taught him of the singing art – 'If you sing any kind of jazz you finally discover it's Armstrong you're imitating. Imitation is no bad thing' – though it should not be overlooked that in his music class Bennett fell in with a group of cantors and found himself utilizing their form of vocal projection, which was part and parcel of the synagogue. He also learnt a great deal when he joined the American Theater Wing's professional school where he studied drama, diction and musical theory. 'I guess that was when Tony Bennett, serious singer, was born. I had a music teacher Miriam Speir and she told me that if I wanted to make popular music to go down to 52nd Street and imitate anyone, not necessarily picking out a vocalist. I did some busking myself and in the bars of saloons of New York I hoped the working-class people who inhabited them would toss the odd dime. When I'm in London and I see the buskers around the Leicester Square cinema queues I get kinda nostalgic! It was a good learning ground.'

A further situation where he learnt of other forms of popular music was in the army. Here he heard and sang soldiers' favourites like 'Sentimental Journey', 'I'll Be Seeing You', and 'Don't Sit under the Apple Tree'.

He was shipped overseas and spent three years with the 63rd Infantry Division in Germany. At the end of the war he was transferred to Special Services, the army entertainment branch, where he says he was given a place in the trumpet section in the augmented dance band from the regimental marching band. 'I couldn't play a note but I used to go through the motions so that I could stay with the band and sing.' In early times Bennett was a prisoner of his own immediate avarice as a performer – he wanted results fast. 'I used to come on and give them something fast, a screamer. But the reaction was bad. I didn't understand it. Then Count Basie explained it to me: "If you start at the top there's nowhere to go." So I learned to pace it, building all the time. It's a dramatic performance – a piece of theatre.'

His shows became known for their cleverness in building pace, and circumstances dictated that it should be so by the time real popularity dawned. He couldn't afford to inject endless energy night after night when on many occasions he would be performing two houses, especially as in clubland the second house would often be in the early hours of morning. He would have been a physical wreck long before middle-age!

Today, the artist takes things in his stride with the deceptive ease of the man who knows he has arrived and can deliver the goods. He saunters on stage, his broad shoulders a landmark, the worn features now part and parcel of a rugged, almost tough-looking person. Few realize that sometimes he has arrived at the theatre only minutes before his curtain call – as he did in Manchester, Britain, 1982 – for he can go right into his act with the suddenness and ease of a finely tuned choir. 'Experience, time, polish, they are what counts. It takes ten years to learn how to walk on stage. There's something very special and individual about the performers the public takes to its heart. I've never forgotten what Anthony told me: "Don't try to compete with anyone else, only with yourself." So that's what I do. I just try to measure up to what I know I can do – and hope it's good enough.'

Back-stage he is friendly, somewhat impersonal, and with him these days there is no entourage of any size; he is aware that for an artist it is always the performance which counts, that people should be pleased. He welcomes genuine reviewers able to express their pleasure at the way he handles all things, from vocal ability and song interpretation to working with an orchestra, band or small-piece outfit: even with years of experience he must still work hard at what he does.

As a performer and individual he demands respect. At times he is exciting, dynamic, possessing the controlled aggression to fire an audience into ecstasy. It is his overall enthusiasm that has attracted many people – his outbursts of joy when something has gone well. These expressions of pleasure have been related solely to music, not to money or charts. In July 1964, for instance, he said he had made his best-ever disc when he recorded 'Danny Boy' with backing from Stan Getz and pianist Hank Jones, 'a backing so cool I was iced-up for the whole session'. And Tony has not been the only enthusiast for particular tracks or albums: many critics have often shown a 'Bennettish' enthusiasm.

Ken Barnes in *Sinatra and the Great Song Stylists* picks the LP *Songs for the Jet Set* as a fine example of Bennett at his undiluted best. He praises Don Costa's electrifying arrangement for orchestra and chorus – replete with Al Cohn's fine tenor sax solo. *Tony Bennett Sings His All-Time 'Hall of Fame Hits'* has a superb ballad montage incorporating 'It Had to Be You' and 'One for My Baby' with fine sensitive piano from John Bunch. Barnes enthuses over Tony's remarkable vocal of Antonio Carlos Jobim's 'Wave' on the 'live' LP *Get Happy with the London Philharmonic*, flips over Tony's title track 'Yesterday I Heard the Rain' and chooses his interpretation of Jerome Kern's 'Remind Me' as one of the high spots of *With Love* but reserves top marks for the sheer delicacy of Tony's phrasing throughout 'Lazy Day in Love' from the same LP. Barnes comments: 'Surely a master craftsman at work.'

'I've had an attitude right from the start, that the only thing to do if I was going to be in show business was to be a full professional. With the right breaks, the right policy, and a certain amount of talent to offer, you'll win in the end. It takes time.' And here he's positive that looks don't count in the balance: 'Before I was a success I was told that I didn't look like a singer, because of this big Roman nose of mine. I was always being told, "Get a nose job." I came really close to having one, too, but a close musician friend was against it, and I thought, "It's not worth losing a friend over." Now I'm glad I didn't change my appearance.' It hasn't stopped the women, that's for sure. Once he was asked for his secret and he told *Daily Express*'s Peter Dacre: 'Music is sex. I suppose I make people dream a while.'

But of course he has adopted one mannerism that has become one of his looked-for trademarks, that of loosening his tie, which he borrowed from Al Jolson. 'With me it's superstition. I'm giving the audience something I've learned from a great artist. It's a nod to the past. I think people like it.' And if anyone should quibble then there's the immediate example of another 'great' who has also borrowed from Jolson – Sinatra has the habit of sauntering on stage and shedding his coat before going into his first number.

Bennett the artist thinks about his audience beyond the sense of 'giving them the goods'. 'I learnt in many varied routes to success that there's no such thing as separate audiences. You're on stage to entertain people. Different age-groups aren't important. I'm aware of how people are feeling. I suppose as an artist I have shifted people toward the so-called 'sunny side of the street' whereas Frank Sinatra has been the singer for the lonely, the outcast, the sad and the bad.' Bennett stresses any artist's need of courage – 'the courage to go out and face a crowd and give it to them, exposing one's innermost emotions. That's what I admire about Paul McCartney. He has courage. No lies when he performs, it eliminates the critics. The other Beatles have a lot of things going for them.' (So he spoke in 1968 but of course sadly Lennon is dead, and the

Beatles live on only in the memory and the incessant run of re-issues and repackaging for the thriving new audience.) And he mentions the value of support from fellow artists. He recalls the friendship shown to him by Frank Sinatra when he was a comparatively new performer.

'Around 1958 Perry Como gave me my biggest chance. I was invited to take over as the summer replacement for his television show and I was so terrified I didn't know whether I should take the job. By chance I met Frank Sinatra. I didn't know him but anyway I felt he might be sympathetic and so I told him my problem, saying I was completely frightened. He said that didn't matter because an audience kind of likes this. He said it meant that I cared which was so much better than being cool and not caring. Sinatra calmed me down quite a bit and I took the job.

'Since then I've got to know him. He's an amazing man, a loner who only likes a few people. He once said that besides himself there were only two singers who mattered – me and Sarah Vaughan. The others were insignificant. It was an astonishing thing to say, when you consider how many fine singers there are, and how offended they'd be by such a remark. But he wouldn't worry.'

Tony refutes those who say he shouldn't sing of the bright and happy. 'Life is a constant shifting of light and shadow, joy and sorrow. I concentrate on the happiness whenever I can, because I like to make others happy. I will not touch anything that invites people to be miserable. I'm aware as the next man that we live in a tough and violent world. But we must try to see the beauty of our world, and look for joy and enjoyment.

'I think many people have been brainwashed into accepting what is thrown out by the commercial world. You know once – when I was a teenager – I realized there was a whole spectrum of music. I liked Gilbert and Sullivan as well as Fats Waller, and Art Tatum. These little Hitlers in the modern music business tried to underplay people like Crosby, Sinatra, Perry Como, Sarah Vaughan, Peggy Lee – and me. They told our kids: "Don't listen, they're not your kind of music."'

Early in the 1970s Tony said he had no other wish than to 'make better and better music – just to keep going upwards'. And a hallmark of his career as an artist has been the care he's taken to choose the right material, and if sometimes he plays safe then there have also been times when he's sung the unexpected. During a typical performance he may well perform numbers from the Gershwin–Kern–Berlin–Arlen standards book – and of course sing 'I Left My Heart in San Francisco' and 'Joanna', but he will occasionally surprise his audience by choosing a tune from the B-side of one of his singles or he may perform Kurt Weill's 'Lost in Stars', giving as a reason: 'It hasn't got a beat and you can't dance to it but I think it says a lot.'

'San Francisco' is described elsewhere in the section on the 1970s but Bennett has said: 'The success of that record changed me. It led to my getting offers from all over the world, and this led to my getting a lot more ambitious. I began working 25 per cent harder and I studied music.'

His entire attitude to his career as an artist is permeated with the desire to search incessantly for perfection – the height of which only he knows.

But of course Bennett, as any other artist in the singing business, is aware that the kind of musical accompaniment he receives can have the most tumultuous effect on what he performs. A successful artist can always grab the best, especially when he tours a foreign country and because of union rules must accept musicians he may not know or have worked with and who have nationality residing with the territory he is visiting. A young up-and-coming performer may have problems but Bennett has been fortunate in finding himself with some exceptional producers and musicians almost from the word go.

Bennett encountered ace-producer Mitch Miller at the outset of his recording career. Miller was one of the record world's 'gods' Stateside and as Arnold Shaw describes in his most excellent book *The Rockin' 50s* the ex-Mercury producer was at the forefront of the enormous number of hit records that came US Columbia's way in the early 1950s.

Miller resided at the Columbia Record Company's offices on 799 Seventh Avenue on the corner of Fifty-second Street and was auditioning by eight in the morning. Miller – apart from his own successes with the Mitch Miller Orchestra and Chorus – had an incredible array of people in his roster: Laine had come over from Mercury, there was Doris Day, Guy Mitchell, Johnnie Ray, the Four Lads, Johnny Mathis, Vic Damone, Rosemary Clooney and Mindy Carson at one time or another in the 1950s and at its outset there was also Tony Bennett.

It was Miller who early in 1951 took the infectious Hank Williams country ballad 'Cold, Cold Heart' and tossed it Tony's way for a cover version. As Shaw writes: 'the man with the chesty baritone' had a hit record.

In the musical stakes Bennett has benefited enormously from his relationship with Ralph Sharon who was born in Britain but has found his musical success across the Atlantic, and who was with Bennett from 1951 onwards. 'There's no doubt that this guy Sharon, who is a truly brilliant arranger and pianist, has influenced my presentation more than somewhat. He's a jazz boy and I guess a lot of my phrasing comes from studying the jazz musicians. Specially guys like Miles Davies, Zoot Sims, Chuck Wayne and Eddie Costa. I "feel" for jazz. That helps.

'He helped me transform myself. He taught me always to insist on working with good musicians and not just work with house bands. He told me to ring up Count Basie and ask to sing with him. But I said I couldn't – I hadn't even met the Count. But Sharon insisted – even though my record company at the time was frightened of me singing jazz. They – thinking of the immediate dollar – said it wasn't commercial. But I took Sharon's advice and now I'm becoming very spoilt, working with the great bands.'

Not unexpectedly, Sharon makes flattering comments on Tony. 'I have never met an artist who is more dedicated to his profession. He has musical integrity – a truly wonderful thing these days of the quick gimmick, "hoked-up" sounds and trick backgrounds.'

Sharon stresses Tony's musical commitment that involves a ceaseless search for perfection and an unwillingness to settle for the quick and easy. 'As Tony's arranger and conductor I find that sometimes we will wind up doing six or seven arrangements of a number before settling for one that "makes it". Whatever arrangement Tony settles for you can be sure that it's the right one for him. And you can be equally sure, too, that the score will have a jazz flavour, because Tony is steeped in jazz.'

Sharon, in mentioning that Tony's supporters in the early days were Sinatra, and Nat 'King' Cole, says the one thing they all admire 'is that Tony never allows his night act to get "set". A stale or static act irritates him, and he is constantly changing, improving, altering songs, switching tempos to keep his performance alive and fresh.'

Jazz is the musical form that allows Tony most variation and Sharon adds: 'The reason he likes a jazz-styled background is that he can build new ideas and find new concepts with this type of musical "carpet".'

Bennett's relationship with the big bands has often led people to question whether Bennett the artist is a jazz singer. It's very noticeable that numerous encyclopaedias on jazz artists make no reference to Bennett in this context; in some sense it sounds like an expression of the awful elitism and snobbery amongst some of the jazz fraternity in their so-called search for purity (witness their views on women singers and the few they admit into the so-called hallowed description of a 'jazz singer') but weighed against this must of course be Bennett's own disclaimer that he is a jazz singer. 'I try not to categorize myself. I never like to publicize the fact; it's something of a stigma to be tagged a jazz singer. I like to sing with a big band, but I like also to consider myself flexible enough to sing with just a piano, trio or quartet.' And as if to verify the authenticity of his statement Bennett has often said that he fulfilled a major ambition of his when he sang in Britain with the London Philharmonic Orchestra.

'Appearing in front of an orchestra of a hundred men was quite a challenge – an entirely different musical concept. But we really swung – and I think we scooped the pop singers in this field. I believe I was the first one to really get it on here. To show what can really be done if you have a feeling for something and know what you want to do.'

He started working with Basie around 1958 and adds: 'It was almost that long ago, too, that I played the Americana Hotel in Florida with Duke Ellington's band. I can't tell you what dates like these meant in terms of musical education. It was a priceless experience for me and my musicians.

'Before that time I had stuck to café jobs mostly with local house bands plus Ralph's rhythm section. But with these bands I got into an entirely different state of mind – and working with Count is very different from working with Duke because one band roars and the other band growls. Woody Herman's band and its spirit always were perfect for me, too.' And in 1965 he said: 'The reason why I played with these bands is twofold. First, as I say, it's musically stimulating; but also, I notice there are so many pessimists in the business today who say nothing is happening. Well, it's easy to disprove that.' And Bennett in this interview, given in 1965, pointed out how Ella Fitzgerald had put together a show in Los Angeles with Tony, the Basie Band and the Oscar Peterson Trio. It was held on a Monday night, the worst evening of the week, and there was Stan Kenton in town holding forth at another theatre, yet Bennett pointed out the house was packed and everyone enjoyed themselves. He thought entertainers should combine and play together a lot more and at this time remarked that Jack Jones or Nancy Wilson with Woody Herman could make an evening to remember.

Ellington has always been one of the artist's idols with Tony saying his favourite Ellington song – written with Billy Strayhorn when the Duke was nineteen – is 'The Lush Life'. But it's a number he doesn't sing in public. 'The late Nat Cole made THE version of that song,' he explains, 'and I wouldn't even try to get near it. I came after the big band era and always felt I missed something. So I became a real fan of the bands, and to this day I collect their records. You know, they're kind of imaginary to me in many cases. I didn't witness a lot of things like the Jimmy Lunceford happenings. I heard about them but I didn't witness them. But I guess I made up for lost time by hanging around some of the greats like Bobby Hackett, Louis Armstrong, Basie and the Duke. I admired tremendously the Ellington outfit,' and back in 1961 the vocalist-artist had hopes of recording with the band: 'For a variety of reasons we've never been able to get together long enough to complete a recording session. You see Ellington is on tour most of the time, and so, for that

44

matter, am I. Still some day we'll get around to it, and I know for sure that recording with Ellington is going to be the greatest kick of all.' Alas, it was not to be.

Derek Witt recalls how he witnessed at first hand the respect Ellington had for Tony.

'I was new at CBS and I was sent over to New York (the headquarters of US Columbia, CBS in the UK). CBS head Ken Glancey told me to make the most of the trip and get some atmosphere. I thought it would be great if I could meet Tony and I left a message. I went out on the town, theatre, dinner and so on and returned to my hotel just before midnight. And went to my room. I rang down because my red light was on and the girl said there had been a couple of messages for me. She said: "You are to call TB." I said that would be Tony Bennett. I remember she gasped and said, "You mean Tony Bennett, the singer." I said, yes it would be.

'So what was I to do? It was late but anyway I phoned Tony. He said: "Get a cab and come over, it's my birthday."'

Witt found Tony relaxed, gentle and laid-back. The penthouse was grand. Tony's wife, Sandy, was there.

'Tony suddenly went click and said to Sandy, "We're going out." I thought it was the case of the bonks!'

Tony said, 'Ellington's in town. We're going over to see the Duke.' Sandy went away and came back extra-glamorous and off we went in a great limo to the club which is found at the top of the RCA building. We were sitting there when Duke came over and the two embraced warmly. I was introduced by Tony: 'This is my buddy from London.' I felt like a twelve-year-old. I was over the moon with pleasure. It was as simple as that. Two great men meeting and me there.'

Bill Evans was another musician with whom Tony wanted to record. In 1977 he told Max Jones of *Melody Maker*: 'Fantastic isn't it? The idea that a jazz musician –

and one like Bill Evans – should want to make records with a singer. It's really a great compliment. And we'll do it someday. We're working it out so that we're not putting any pressure on ourselves. When we're in the same town we'll do two to three sides and over the years finally put it together.'

Other ambitions at the time were 'to record again with Basie, the Harry James and Les Brown bands'. In terms of Bennett the jazz-influenced artist, the most interesting LP release at this time was *The Beat of my Heart*, where he was supported by some of America's leading instrumental soloists.

Another person much valued in his career is trumpeter Bobby Hackett whose artistry has provided many delicious backgrounds, especially for ballads. Hackett has said: 'Tony has only the choice repertoire. He's a very fine artist. And, believe me, I'm not saying it just because I work with him. He's a musician at heart. He likes to swing and pick his spots' (meaning the people he worked with and the chosen venue). Hackett – famed for being one of the best horn men in jazz – could blow a brief but beautiful passage whenever Bennett asked, or so it seemed.

But how do fans see Tony? Undoubtedly they would join with the critical appraisal of those who have put pen to paper and described his musical work, and like the huge majority of such people they glow with positive warmth at the mention of the singer. However, there are those who see qualities in Bennett beyond the confines of vocal artistry and pleasing sound. Laurie Henshaw in *Melody Maker*, early in the 1970s, found there were those who dug Bennett's 'masculinity' or as one fan put it: 'You know he's a man. Singers like Johnny Mathis and Nat "King" Cole are OK as background listening, but when I want to do some smoochy dancing, I like to listen to Tony Bennett.'

Henshaw quoted the 'masculinity' term to Tony and was told: 'I think youngsters appreciate any artist who believes in what he is doing. I don't try and project an image. If I have a "gimmick" it's that I don't have a "gimmick". I try to be myself.'

One thing he has not done as an artist is actively to identify himself with causes, though of course his 'charity work' does give him a relationship with groups and organizations busily trying to aid the unfortunate. He does not sing political or social songs. But because he does not preach through his music it does not mean he is unconcerned. He says he has never lost an awareness of what it is to walk the streets, shuffling in the cold. He is aware of the tough lives many people lead, but social and political convictions are a private matter.

'I'm a humanist, I think that's the simplest way of putting it. I am anti-fascist, anti-war, anti-violence of whatever kind. The destruction you know, it's all so heartless and pointless. I'm a great supporter of world citizenry – break down the barriers and let everybody go where they will. Nationalism is such an awful thing. Why can't we realize that there's enough for us all to go round if only we share it fairly? Life is a beautiful thing.'

When he was asked by Gordon Burns for *Radio Times*, whether he would support his own sons in their evasion of the draft he replied: 'All the way. In fact, I'd say that's exactly what I've brought them up to do. I've taught them to hate war like me. I was an infantryman for three years myself and I know exactly what goes on. Pablo Casals once told me that people in our positions must use our influence to *combat* the politicians who the people no longer trust. I'm prepared to talk in an interview like this, but barn-storming is not my scene. The only time I get up on a platform is to sing.' And on his singing in relation to his records Bennett doesn't give house room to his own records.

'I don't want to imitate the way I sound on another record. Every song is different and you sing it differently. I don't want to get into the habit of singing everything the same way.'

It's doubtful if he could.

3.

Painter Man: On And Off Duty

TONY WAS A FAN of Billie Holiday. She made a great impact on him: 'Not because she was "singing jazz". She was singing Billie. She was singing her life.' His remark was made against the backcloth of those who wanted to categorize him. 'It just happens that when the greatest American musicians play or sing, when they're dedicated performers, dedicated to their own talents, to honest emotion, to communication, then what they play or sing gets to be called "jazz". It's too limiting a word. It implies that they're all doing the same thing and they're not. Every one of them is different from everyone else.' And while the question of whether he is or is not a jazz singer sometimes comes his way – and was discussed in the previous chapter – this reaction against classification had a deeper motivation.

Right from his early student days he had always been interested in 'art' and if singing stole his love and commitment when he was in his late teens and early twenties he later experienced a gradual pull towards painting. Since the 1960s painting has assumed considerable importance and some would even dare say that in the 1980s it has equalled if not overtaken singing as Tony's primary method of self-expression. But even before the 1980s he was prepared to be described both as a singer and an artist and certainly his achievements as a painter show that he is no mere amateur passing the time of day in a relaxing fashion with brush and canvas. But to some degree his interest in painting seems to fit in with the generally shy demeanour of a man whose opinions are more often than not expressed without flamboyance or extravagant gestures, in contradiction to the image suggested by his plumb-line nose and protruding jaw!

Bennett – the man with success on a palette – has even moved into that rather select class of artists whose work is commissioned for considerable sums (in his case in excess of $200,000). He has passed from painting as a hobby into more rarefied and refined circles. He told *Daily Express* writer Adella Lithman that for one landscape painted from his window in New York he had received £6,000 but, as the extremely attractive lady reporter added, 'For one concert performance Tony Bennett gets £10,000 a night!' His painting of Williamsburg Bridge was bought for $11,000 by the Franklin Mint, Philadelphia, and a limited edition of prints was sold for roughly the same amount.

Apart from the financial side – a subject about which Bennett is reticent (he once said, 'I won't say how much I earn because there's an awful lot of people not making as much as me and I don't want to offend them') – he likes to draw a close cosy comparison between singing and art. His paintings hang in an assortment of art galleries, including New York's Lincoln Center, and though there remains some doubt as to just how many of his works have been completed a figure approaching two hundred – and certainly more than 150 – seems reasonable. He both paints and sketches scenes as he travels and also paints portraits, often of famous people. These include Count Basie, Duke Ellington, Bette Davies and Jimmy Cagney; but at the other extreme he has painted many an unknown restaurant waiter. He has been assembling what he terms 'a pictorial autobiography. I thought I'd call it Songs and Sketches, or Benetto Paints Tony Bennett.'

In 1977 he had his first British art exhibition at a leading Mayfair gallery in London. Fifty works were exhibited; paintings in oils and acrylics and pen and ink drawings, with subject matter ranging from his cat Ophelia to city scenes. He said at the time, 'You see, I've got two careers now. When one gets too hectic I get over the other. It's good relief. Art is completely opposite to the stage, where I get immediate reaction to my work. With painting it's severe concentration and it's so private. Most people who pay to hear me sing, like my singing. But some people who see my art work either think it's terrible or beautiful. I like that. It's stimulating.'

Bennett told how art and musical talent were also to be found in his two oldest boys: 'We're of Italian descent and music and art are our heritage. You (British) have got the theatre and literature, and the Germans have science. You see, painting and singing have a lot in common – they both have line, form, colour and balance.'

His British visit in March 1982 for a ten-city tour saw a private buyer offer him £80,000 to complete a series of four pictures. Venezuela, Greece and Scotland were the countries that offered appropriate scenery, with San Francisco also suggesting itself. 'It has been a good city to me,' he said on one occasion during the visit. 'I just can't stop drawing and painting. Everywhere I go I sketch – much of it, of course, rooftop scenes because I spend so much time in hotel rooms.' So oils, canvas and easel have become regular travelling companions, and offers have come his way from galleries on both sides of the water. 'You know I'm happy that people like my painting but it's not vital. I have public approval (as in music, so in art, personal integrity first, the rest can follow) and I can't in truth say I'm all that good, not yet, anyway. I paint simply because of the peace . . . a feeling of calm I get when I have completed a canvas. Painting gets rid of all the frustrations in me. It gives me a sense of peace and that's why I like my paintings to reflect tranquillity.'

He told showbusiness expert Roderick Gilchrist of the *Daily Mail* that his favourite subject was man in relation to nature. 'A yacht sailing on the sea, or people in the park or a lady beside a vase of flowers.'

He said to Gilchrist that oil painting had achieved two things for him. The first was the acquisition of discipline. 'Before, when I used to do stuff I didn't like, I'd rip it up and start again. What you have to do is look at your mistake, analyse it, then paint around it until you get the line right.' Bennett told Gilchrist that the second thing he had learnt was an awareness of how blind he had formerly been. He now knew that so many beautiful things were waiting to be seen and sensed.

'Painting has opened my eyes to sights that were always there but I never really noticed. How many times do any of us look at a daffodil or a hedgerow?' Bennett says that a prospective painter must look, observe and mentally retain an image if he is to be successful. 'This examination of nature has awakened me to many beautiful sights. It's as if a fog has been lifted from in front of me. I'm seeing the whole world again through new eyes and it looks just beautiful, from where I'm sitting. Just beautiful.'

Gilchrist said his conversation with Bennett ranged through many periods of art, with the singer showing a tremendous knowledge of art history. But while Tony might talk of the great art movements and the famous names of painting he had a knack of coming down to earth and in personal reflections recalled many pieces of advice he had been given at one time or another. 'At art school one of my instructors gave me a piece of advice: "You must work every day at your art."' And this is what he does – as far as it is humanly possible. But painting has not been Bennett's only interest outside singing. Once he talked of buying some land in England with the intention of turning it into a Bonanza-style ranch, with the surrounding countryside made into an exclusive holiday resort for rich Americans.

Bennett has said that there is nowhere else in the world which has such wonderful countryside as England and the singer suggested that his ranch could feature outdoor sports, such as shooting, fishing, swimming and golf. One rather original and somewhat startling suggestion was this: 'Each American visitor will have his very own English butler.' But nothing came of the project.

His own living quarters Stateside have often been distinct and individualistic. In 1965 he was living in a comfortable New Jersey home with two acres of Japanese landscaping, the place he called 'Next Day Hill'.

Other interests of his have included photography, tinkering with hi-fidelity products, tape equipment and listening to other singers. But interestingly enough he doesn't give house room to his own records. Certainly Tony Bennett has the wealth to pursue almost any interest which is within his range but like many with capital his tastes remain relatively unambitious though always expressed – like his music – with taste and charm.

But wealth does not offer an instant passport to any kind of happiness let alone a lasting relationship and the private life of Bennett – which he has guarded jealously though not with total success from a prying media – has not been without mishaps, mainly in the marital stakes. Bennett has been married twice and both marriages eventually fell apart. Each produced two children, the first boys and the second girls.

Tony's first marriage in 1952 reflected the hysteria that surrounded a singer's lifestyle in those times. His reputed fan club of 200,000 members showed little enthusiasm and many turned up at his wedding in mourning. Wife number-one was blonde model Patricia Beech and their parting was accompanied by a testy divorce case (the suit was filed in 1967) which was well covered by the press.

Patricia obtained a decree on account of the singer's desertion. An adultery charge against Bennett – then forty-five-years-old – was filed by Patricia, naming singer Sandra Grant and claiming that Miss Grant was expecting Bennett's child but the allegation was not pursued. It had been alleged that Miss Grant and Bennett committed adultery on 31 December 1966 in an apartment in Manhattan and also 'in the months and years before and after' that date. She said the singer left her on 19 August 1964 and 'wilfully, continuously and obstinately' deserted her. The final witness was the couple's seventeen-year-old-son. D'Andrea testified that his father walked out of the spacious $60,000 family home in Englewood, New Jersey, in 1964 and never returned.

Bennett lived with Sandy for some years before finally marrying her. In 1968 he said: 'When my divorce does come through, I will marry this girl' and blonde Sandi (the more intimate of the two spellings that followed her), who was an actress as well as singer, said in March 1968: 'I've thrown my career up because Tony is such a groovy man.' Sandi, who came from Louisiana, had had her former marriage dissolved eight years previously.

In January 1962 Bennett announced he was the proud father of a new baby girl – born out of wedlock. The press was not slow to point out that he and Sandi had joined Mia Farrow, Mick Jagger, Vanessa Redgrave and Andre Previn in becoming parents without bothering to become Mr and Mrs first. The child, Joanna, weighed in at six pounds. Bennett, forty-two and Sandi, twenty-nine, looked more than pleased with the event.

A year later the couple's unmarried state gave rise to newspaper gossip that Bennett's solo appearance for drinks with Prince Philip at Buckingham Palace was due to his not being married. But in an interview with Lynda Lee Potter, the silky, ash-blonde Sandi, then aged thirty, discounted the story that her invitation had been withdrawn once it was realized the two were not Mr and Mrs. She said the invitation had never included her. The former actress said: 'I got Tony because I made myself available. I was introduced to him by friends. I fell in love with him and I just cancelled everything. When he went to New York and stayed in a hotel, I followed him. I figured if I didn't get him, somebody else would. It's kind of tough now travelling around with the baby, and I just don't know how I'll manage when she goes to school. I'd never stay behind though. The only way our relationship works for me is to travel everywhere with him. When I was pregnant, because of our legal circumstances, I thought about having an abortion but I just couldn't do it. When I told Tony, he was happy for me because he knew how much I wanted his child.'

Sandi told Lynda that her mother knew everything though she sometimes got upset. 'I tell her that I'm just as married as her small-time friends who criticize me to her all the time. I wear a wedding ring because I feel married. I feel taken even if I don't have a piece of paper. I'm very possessive and I don't want other girls flirting or making passes.'

Ms Grant told how she disliked other girls attempting to flirt with Tony and how they sometimes even entered their hotel room, whereupon she would order them out. 'If I see a threat I try and take care of it right in the beginning. I try always to be around. Many times a man is unfaithful because the opportunity is there. If something is thrown at a man he usually takes advantage of it.'

Eventually the Bennett – Beech divorce case was settled by Superior Court Judge August Hackman with Patricia Bennett rumoured to have been awarded £36,000 a year. And Tony and Sandie (a later spelling) were finally married – in secret – on the first Tuesday of 1972 at City Hall, New York. The arrangement was not favoured by the press who only caught the whiff and scent of a likely event.

Public relations firm Tony Barrow International said that the singer admitted keeping the news from the American press for six days. The marriage was announced in Britain by Tony Bennett himself. 'We decided to announce our marriage in Britain, because we're very fond of this country. Being married has lifted a lot of tension from us.' And new wife Sandie added: 'Most people Tony and I met in the last few years have been understanding about our situation.'

By 1973 Tony was extolling the marriage. 'My marriage is now a marvellous relationship. Sandie and I have a great relationship with great understanding. There really aren't any rules about marriage, no matter how much society says there are. Some of the rules are, I think, very hypocritical. The great thing is to have peace of mind. If you have that you have a great thing going. Love is the answer. Without that we just shrivel up and merely exist. Love comes in different ways to different people. Thank God I've found my way with Sandie and Joanna.'

But three years later show-business gossip suggested that all was not entirely well. Several press stories circulated. In one, Sandie, now a mother of two – Joanna and two-year-old Antonia – said 'My life seems empty save for two screaming kids. Sometimes I really miss New York and its excitement. Tony's happy. He loves California.'

Tony said: 'Sure I miss California when I'm away. But I miss Sandie too, when she isn't with me. She makes it sound as if we're quarrelling all the time. In fact, there's a lot of love between us.'

But Sandie was then quoted as adding: 'Tony makes it sound like a perfect marriage but we've had our share of fights. Sometimes I can be awfully rough on him.'

In another interview Tony's wife professed her worry over the marriage. 'I'm tough but very scared. This marriage has been my whole life and this marriage can go either way. But it will have to change if we're going to make it.' She talked of a Tony who was shy and humble on stage but who could be a 'screamer' when they quarrelled. 'I felt he didn't take strong enough action to bring about the divorce from his first marriage. Only when his career is concerned does he take a strong position; otherwise he just hopes or expects the problem to go away.' She called Tony the most insecure man she had ever met. 'It was very appealing at first. He was so vulnerable. Soon you find it is taking all your energy. You become a slave to it.' The singer's wife talked further of the effect his career was having upon her attitude to sex. Much of the material culled by newspapers came from an American book, *Are You Anybody?* by Marilyn Funt, and in other extracts, from an impartial point of view, the Bennetts marriage looked even rockier. Sandie Bennett was instanced as a beautiful blonde who fell for the handsome crooner sixteen years ago and was now an embittered wife who couldn't sleep at nights. 'Our marriage can't go on like this indefinitely. It has to change for us to make it.'

When Sandie appeared alone at three parties and he failed to make her birthday celebrations the gossips had a field day and obviously something was terribly wrong. Newspaper columns were filled with the story of Sandie, now forty, two-stepping with sixty-eight-year-old Gene Kelly while Tony was linked with Filipino beauty thirty-eight-year-old Minda Feliciano. The two were reported to be setting up home in swish trendy Rodeo Drive, seen as the Mayfair of Beverley Hills, Los Angeles. Minda had a teenage son through her marriage to Leo Guild, who had written a biography of Hedy Lamarr entitled *Extasy And Me*.

Tony has commented: 'I really would have liked a "marriage made in heaven" and a good family life. But this business I'm in doesn't help that kind of thing. With

57

all the travel involved, there's just no sense of continuity. A woman who wants to stay at home, well, she just can't be happy with someone who lives out of a suitcase.'

Bennett feels that his failed marriages represent a flaw in the story of his career but at least he has the compensation of four splendid children and a reputation for kindness and generosity to all and sundry. Some would say he changed after his second marriage and that his overall attitude toward the business altered. They suggest that it was partially responsible for his break with the family record company Columbia – CBS and others add that it has meant he spends less and less time with fellow musicians. But whatever the pros and cons of people's evaluations there is little dispute that, off-stage, Tony can be most personable and pleasurable company. His work for charities has been outlined elsewhere but one story seems pertinent. CBS Corporate Publicity Manager, Derek Witt recalls how Bennett played a major role in raising money for the dependents of a London policeman who was shot early in the 1970s.

'There was a Trust Fund established and a special concert was arranged for Hammersmith Town Hall. Tony was here on holiday and not playing concerts. CBS was called and I was contacted to see whether I could persuade Tony to help out. I said no. I mean it seemed unfair, the man was here to relax. I had a call from the BBC and they said they were interested and thought how it would make a good outside broadcast. I thought some more about it and began to feel I might have made a mess of it.

'Eventually I went over to see Tony at the hotel where he was staying. While I was there the phone rang. Tony said "You take it, Derek." So I did and blow me if it wasn't the chap who had approached me and was obviously persistent and had somehow got hold of Tony's hotel location and through to his room. Well, Tony now wanted to know what this was all about so I told him. To my pleasure and everyone else's he agreed to do the gig, even though really he was here to rest. He did four or five numbers. The funny thing was this – at the concert no-one had remembered to tell compere David Jacobs and I remember someone rushing back-stage and saying Tony was on and saying, "I haven't told David Jacobs, he doesn't know Tony's up on stage pretty soon." But it was a marvellous gesture from Tony – it's the kind of person he is.'

The view seems to be universal.

PART TWO

4.

First Days

THE BABY BORN on Long Island, New York, 3 August 1926 was not christened Tony Bennett. The child was known as Anthony Dominick Benedetto.

Anthony was born into an Italian immigrant family in the lean days of the 1920s. His father, Giomanni Benedetto emigrated to the States in 1907 from a small Italian town near Reggio, in Calabria. He met his wife Anna Suraci in New York City. A tailor by trade, Giomanni found a living in another field when with his sister and her husband, he established a popular grocery shop on the corner of Sixth Avenue and 43rd Street. The chosen site – by one of those strange coincidences – became the headquarters of the US record Company giant Columbia and it was this company that was to sign Tony Bennett, singer.

Anthony Dominick was the youngest in a family of three. He had a sister called Mary, five years older than himself, and an older brother, John. Undoubtedly the Benedetto family found life far from easy but there seems little truth in the popular journalistic myth that he was born in a New York slum and that his family was poor, not knowing where the next cent or dime was coming from. The Long Island family of Benedetto suffered their biggest blow when Giomanni died. Tony was a mere child of nine and his mother was forced to find a living. She did so by working as a seamstress, a job she held for seventeen years. The housework was done by Mary.

'I appreciated only too well the efforts and sacrifices my mother would make. I was resolved that one day I would make big money and be able to provide a comfortable life for her. The saddest day of my life was when my father died. But my father lived long enough to pass on to me his great love of music. We're of Italian stock, so it's not surprising that music should always have been an important part of our family life.' When he was three Anthony was taken by his father to see the film *Sonny Boy* and some days later, covered completely in white powder, he made a theatrical entrance before the family and proclaimed, 'Me, Sonny Boy': the family were highly amused and none more so than father Giomanni, an avid Jolson fan, and Tony's aunt, whose powder box had supplied the necessary make-up.

He was six when he made his first public debut. Along with his brother he sang a duet, 'Marching along Together', at a ceremony to mark the opening of the Triborough Bridge by New York's Mayor La Guardia. And with Mary and John he regularly brought gasps of appreciation and pleasure from parents at the frequent family music occasions. John had studied music formally and had sung in the children's chorus of the Metropolitan Opera.

Tony's next recorded public appearance saw him singing for an Irish minstrel show! This surprise mix of the son of an Italian family with the Irish community came about because the Irish were the predominant ethnic group in the Astoria area of Long Island where the Benedettos lived. Anthony imitated Eddie Cantor singing Ida.

Not surprisingly he speaks of taking part in other neighbourhood events, musical occasions at the local Roman Catholic Church, school functions and various similar productions, but if he was busy with and interested in singing he did have a greater love – art. 'I had singing lessons in my teens but I also wanted to have art lessons and eventually I did. I was very young when I earned some money by singing in small clubs and the monies I got enabled me to pay for tuition in both spheres.'

But this dual interest posed the early and continuing question as to whether he might choose one of these talents for his future career and if so, then which one should he select as his favourite occupation? He was highly talented in both fields so it could not be a question of choosing the one he was best at. He earned fifteen dollars a week and to supplement this he also worked as a library attendant and the all-time favoured job for out of work or underpaid entertainers – a theatre usher. As a teenager he liked all kinds of music but in interviews he was quick to say 'the best of all kinds'. He was grateful for having heard so many quality artists from an early age and within the warm environment of a friendly home, something only marred by the sad death of his father. And it was a family which was constantly buzzing with some kind of happening, while giving him the vital personal background which proved more than valuable when the young Tony Bennett had to battle his way through initial media exposure.

'I enjoy talking when the company is good and everyone's honest with each other. Talk of that sort is communication and too many people are afraid to communicate, or don't know how, or don't really want to. My whole life is an attempt to communicate.' But as his singing career developed there was one aspect of it that had an oddity known also to fans of Johnny Mathis: 'Maybe it seems strange, therefore, that I don't do much talking when I'm singing. The message gets across when I sing, or else it doesn't. In any case, talking won't change it one way or the other, so why take up people's time with talking when they've paid to hear me sing?'

But a career as a vocalist had to wait a while for Europe

and the Far East were at war and Anthony was needed by his country.

In 1944 he received his US Army service call-up and for three years he was saved from making any career decisions while he served with the 63rd Infantry Division stationed in Germany. Bennett says his army experience gave him a social conscience. 'I was in the infantry in France and Germany and, aside from wondering why people were shooting at each other, I couldn't avoid seeing ridiculous incongruities. When we arrived in Mannheim, for instance, it was a shock to see the whole town flattened, all those humble little homes, and then to look up and see that the Ford plant had been left alone during the bombings.'

In another anecdote from his army days Bennett remembers how he invited an old school friend Frank Smith to dine with him. During the meal an officer from the South of the United States came across and told Bennett that the place for his black friend to eat was the kitchen. Bennett took the request with the respect it deserved which led to his being reduced to private from corporal and finding himself with the unenviable task of digging up soldiers' bodies from mass graves and laying them in individual coffins. After the Second World War was ended he spent time with the Entertainments Branch. He toured army bases and it was here that he encountered pianist Fred Katz who later accompanied Lena Horne, though more relevant to this is the fact that it was Katz who introduced Bennett to his first manager. When his service days were completed Tony stayed on in Germany and for a short period he studied music and art at Heidelberg University – at least an academic set-up gave him the chance to pursue both artistic callings without having to decide which would be his major bread-earner.

Soon after that he was given an ex-serviceman's grant

and back in the States he became a student at the American Theater Wing, later the Actor's Studio, in New York. His coach for singing was Miriam Speir and he was fortunate in meeting someone whose musical tastes were catholic and who saw no reason why he should not hear jazz amidst a wider ranging diet of straight music. 'Often Miriam would point down the street where jazz stars like Coleman Hawkins, Erroll Garner and Art Tatum were playing. "Listen to the way they phrase," she would tell me. "If you can do the same sort of thing in your singing, you'll hit the top one day."' He revelled in the results of such advice and from an early age learnt much about vocal technique, an ability to handle a microphone, and the art of timing. He was also able to hear these and other artists during some of the best days of their careers which later generations could only hear on records. He hoped for a show-business break but nonetheless pursued his craftsmanship in industrial art. But the 'chance' came for him through the efforts of Ray Muscarella when he was offered a spot in a TV talent show hosted by popular American entertainer of the time Arthur Godfrey. He came second. The winner was Rosemary Clooney. 'My bad luck turned to good. I wound up with a contract on another TV show, *Songs for Sale*. Fellow song seller? Rosemary Clooney again! It started me off with my motto for life: "The harder you work, the luckier you become." I've proved it. So much happened for me after this and looking back I've seen that each new project that comes along stimulates and gives me great personal happiness when I can really achieve what I want to do. Life to me, as a songwriter, singer, entertainer, actor and hopeful producer, plus artist, is just one big exciting challenge!'

However the really big break had yet to come and when it did involved America's great son, Bob Hope, who as it happens is British by birth! He was seen by the great star singing in a New York night club and Bob Hope came back stage and told the youthful Anthony: 'You're a fine performer. I'd like you to sing a couple of numbers in my show at the Paramount Theatre.' Stars shone before the amazed Bennett who could hardly stand – such was the effect of the stunning but incredible news he was receiving from the great man.

But after all he hadn't struggled selling newspapers, working in cafés and theatres to lose such an opportunity and he readily accepted. He couldn't have known at the time that he was due for a name-change, for with due respect to his family Anthony Dominick Benedetto was hardly the kind of snappy credit with which to adorn theatre signs or posters let alone hoardings. Hope had the answer and he would give it on stage when Tony came to make his debut at the Paramount.

The theatre was jammed on the night when Anthony was launched on an unsuspecting public who would not grasp at the time that they were in at the start of the career of a vocalist who was to become one of America's all-time greats.

Hope came to the microphone and the audience sensed there was something different that evening in store: 'I'm glad to tell you I've booked this promising singer Anthony Benedetto for my next tour of America.' And next came the news to more than interest Anthony: 'Also, though he doesn't know it yet, his name from now on is going to be Tony Bennett!'

It was a moment which Bennett was never to forget and he was later to marvel at the fact that Hope had originally come to the club to hear Pearl Bailey and had only by chance caught his act.

A new name in show business had been born and this one, unlike most, would not die.

Pearl Bailey would later become a firm friend of Tony's and indeed a welcome visitor to his home; someone who gave valuable advice to his sons as they set out to conquer the pop world. Friendship with popular music's aristocracy, however, would come later, though having won Bob Hope's affection was, to say the very least, a good start in this sphere.

Tony's singing efforts on the Bob Hope Show won rapturous applause from the audience who began queueing to hear this new artist. And Bennett on tour with the entertainer met a similar response, no mean feat in itself as any support artist can testify since audiences can either not bother to leave the bar for a concert's first half or they can give that particular act a cool reception, seeing it as a 'nuisance' to be got through before they can enjoy the main reason why they have paid out their ticket money.

His adoption by Hope was the plus factor that alerted record companies, with Columbia, under the aegis of producer Mitch Miller, winning the race. Tony sent a test pressing of 'Boulevard Of Broken Dreams' by one mail and had a contract by return. Soon he would be recording, with 'gold' discs awaiting, and, once his talent was given mass dissemination on the gramophone record, American music lovers knew a new star had arrived for the 1950s. His successes in the early 1950s were to prove how untrue was the rather incredulous remark made of him in April 1950 that he was just 'another cherubic Italian mama's boy, with a bad case of frogs'. Soon people were to say that he was the natural successor to the king of song, Frank Sinatra.

5.

Through the 1950s–60s: Into This Kingdom He Came

IN TERMS OF music the 1950s in the US were the rockin' years but they were also the period when some balladeers managed either to continue in their familiar style or subtly adapt their material and in this way retain the affections of their fans. The survivors were few in number but Bennett was one.

The early start of the decade, from 1950 to 1951 saw the demise of Tin Pan Alley and has been termed by renowned American writer Arnold Shaw 'the Death of an Era'. It was the prelude to a new order of things which was ushered in on the shoulders of a rather aged musical figure named Bill Haley, the new movement becoming known as 'rock 'n roll'. It was a time when a gulf opened up between teenagers and their parents and the growing affluence of the former was beginning Stateside to spawn a vast industry devoted to culling their monies. True songwriting was soon due to suffer some sledgehammer blows and the artist would become more important than the 'song'. It was the last-gasp-time for high sales of sheet music while the gramophone record was gaining in popularity and the 'live' musician would soon find his or her livelihood threatened by recorded music.

But the change was not unexpected for the new teenagers despaired of the dance bands and wanted something more in tune with their own energies. The world was recovering from the aftermath of World War II and it was obvious the 1950s could not ape the war-infected 1940s or relate to the bygone era of the 1930s.

Britain was much slower to experience change, mainly because in popular musical terms she was subservient to the States. Her main recording artists busily watched the US releases, and 'cover' versions abounded as acts put onto disc their version of an existing US hit. And following the usual pattern rock 'n roll was imported into Britain from across the Atlantic. There was no simultaneous outbreak and it was not surprising really. Rock 'n roll was a popularized amalgam of R & B and Country and Western, and Britain heard little of this, for the BBC, the only outlet for pop music, was not geared to teenage tastes nor, seemingly, did it wish to create them. These were snobbish times and the new music was outlawed by the old established musical fraternity. The only black music to be heard in Britain came from Radio Luxembourg over its wide-ranging transmitters and was popularized by DJs like Tony Hall. In any case British kids were relatively poor and far from possessing the affluence of their American counterparts.

At worst the black music was seen in racial terms but many of the young teenagers in America and later elsewhere were little concerned with such descriptions. And in any case, the kids used the term 'rock 'n roll' to describe the new music. This term was generally seen as coming from famed American DJ, Alan Freed, a white guy who thought a new way of describing the music would make it more acceptable. Freed was in his late twenties and had by chance found himself behind a microphone with the task of spinning conventional pop music as sung by the likes of Nat 'King' Cole, Perry Como, Frank Sinatra, Rosemary Clooney, Bing Crosby and of course Tony Bennett.

The 'family' heard the show and Freed did nothing exceptional but he moved to Cleveland where he was to utter the immortal words 'rock 'n roll' and suddenly kids were queueing to buy the music of black artists.

Freed was the DJ who gave the music a radio airing and he and the radio station found a new audience formed simply and solely of kids – the 'family' monopoly had been broken. Kids were to love the new music and many parents would come to loathe it. Freed was to move East and find radio airtime for the new music in New York and while he stole the DJ 'crown' for the dawning musical era it was of course Haley, who had had a country and western background, who was to steal the record-sales crown. Haley had been recording in the early part of the 1950s, winning some notice for songs like 'Rock the Joint' and 'Shake, Rattle and Roll'. He was charting in the US Top 40 by the end of 1954 with 'Dim, Dim The Lights (I Want Some Atmosphere)', with 'Mambo Rock' and 'Birth of the Boogie' to follow – rather small affairs compared with his fourth US hit, the chart topper '(We're Gonna) Rock Around the Clock'.

All this activity threatened the Bennetts of the 1950s. Bennett had achieved his first million seller in 1952 with the Arthur Hammerstein (uncle of the famed lyricist Oscar Hammerstein)–Dudley Wilkinson composition 'Because of You', which had had its first airing and sales the previous year. He was listed by Arnold Shaw as being in the first division of male balladeers and the list was long: 'Sinatra, Como, Vic Damone, Al Martino, Jerry Vale, Eddie Fisher, Frankie Laine, Alan Dale, Don Cornel, Billy Eckstine, Johnnie Ray, Guy Mitchell, Johnny Desmond, Mario Lanza, and Dean Martin. And a goodly proportion of them were Italian.' As Shaw points out, their musical backing was an 'undercurrent of swirling strings, woollen woodwinds, and light rhythm,' which Shaw says led one adverse critic to see the style as 'the out-of-tempo, rustle-of-spring-sound'. Shaw says with all the Italians around it was no surprise that mainstream pop was a 'pasta of Neapolitan, bel canto, pseudooperatic singing'. Bennett was seen by the writer as belonging with the so-called 'shouters' with Fisher, Cornel and Guy Mitchell, from the previous listing among them and in addition Al Hibbler, Roy Hamilton, the Four Lads and the Ames Brothers. Their female compatriots included Teresa Brewer, Kay Starr, the McGuire Sisters, Rosemary Clooney and Georgia Gibbs. The 'shouters' contrasted with the 'emoters and exhibitionists' like Johnnie Ray and Jackie Wilson, while singer Frankie Laine managed to embody both strains.

Stateside the 1950s had opened with a string of a million selling songs. There was the first million seller for Teresa Brewer with the Weiss–Baum song 'Music Music Music'. Joe, Gene, Vic and Ed, who constituted the Ames Brothers, rode high with their 'Rag Mop' for Coral Records, and while the brothers bounced through that number they found considerable selling power in the flip side, a slowish melodic number entitled 'Sentimental Me'. Ivory Joe Hunter, son of a preacher, went country for 'I Almost Lost My Mind' and his composition received further uplift later in the decade when Pat Boone hit six-figure sales in 1956. The Country and Western chart gave a number-one spot during 1950 to 'The Shot Gun Boogie' from Tennessee Ernie Ford and four of Al Jolson's greatest songs made up a million-selling EP for Decca under the title of *Songs He Made Famous*.

There were the familiar names around – Bing Crosby for one. He joined with son Gary and Matty Matlock's All Stars Orchestra for 'Sam's Song'. The great Nat 'King' Cole with the splendid Les Baxter Orchestra sang 'Mona Lisa', a number featured in the film *Captain Carey*. Billy Eckstine hit the million with the film title song 'My Foolish Heart' and the legendary Weavers along with another marvellous arranger and conductor Gordon Jenkins came up with 'Good Night, Irene'. Patti Page sang

'Tennessee Waltz' and made history with its multi-voiced recording. Three million copies were sold over the counter in 1950 and by 1967 some six million sales had accumulated. There was 'My Heart Cries For You' from Guy Mitchell and the memorable Frankie Laine had his fifth million seller with the haunting 'Cry of the Wild Goose'. Tenor Mario Lanza sang 'Be My Love' from the film *Toast of New Orleans* in which he co-starred with Kathryn Grayson. Lyricist supreme Sammy Cahn wrote the words and Nicholas Brodszky the music. Less noticed amidst all these million sellers was Bennett's first hit 'Boulevard of Broken Dreams' which had come out of his first recording sessions for US Columbia in April 1950.

For Bennett his hit was welcome relief. He had tried many things including covering country music numbers. 'I tried everything from being a race singer to doing Mario Lanza. Then we decided to get some strings and I would just sing sincerely and honestly.'

It was famed US arranger and conductor Percy Faith who suggested he recorded the music hall melody. Shaw thought it was a version that was an echo of Lanza.

The following year saw Tony Bennett achieve his first million seller. He was joined in the official lists for such success by Leroy Anderson, Eddy Arnold, Fred Astaire with Jane Powell, The Four Aces and Red Foley. Better remembered would be the song which established Rosemary Clooney as a major pop force, 'Come-On-A My House'. Wistfully and tender Nat 'King' Cole sang 'Too Young'; Perry Como had a ninth million goodie thanks to 'If'; Doris Day sang 'A Guy Is A Guy', and for sheer emotive excitement there was a double smash from Johnnie Ray, as together with the Four Lads, he came up with 'Cry' and 'Little White Cloud that Cried'. And of course Frankie Laine collected a few million sales with 'Jealousy' and 'Rose, Rose I Love You', with the latter also featuring the Norman Luboff Choir. A major artist was launched into the big-time when 'Indian Love Call' – sung by Slim Whitman who stemmed from Tampa, Florida – hit six-figure sales. Les Paul and Mary Ford as well as Patti Page sold a million a-piece for songwriter Vaughan Horton, with the former bringing their multi-track electric-guitar into prominence.

Tony's hit 'Because of You' had come from the film *I Was an American Spy* and without in any way denigrating the hit it was very much part of the pre-Haley, pre-Presley era.

Tony had two million sellers listed for 1953 and during the middle of 1952 between his first and second million records, the music-and-record-buying public had bought such numbers as Frankie Laine's Western film title track 'High Noon' and his 'Sugar Bush' duet with Doris Day. Peggy Lee recorded one of the great cuts of music history with 'Lover', which had in a somewhat different form been a favourite of early 1930s filmgoers in the Maurice Chevalier/Jeanette MacDonald film *Love Me Tonight*.

Fats Domino gave further notice of interest in rhythm and blues with his second million seller 'Goin' Home'; first-generation Italian–American Al Martino generated emotion with 'Here in My Heart', and for Bennett and other balladeers there was a sign of things to come with nineteen-year-old New Orleans-born Lloyd Price raunching on 'Lawdy, Miss Clawdy', a number which was later to interest the great Elvis Presley. But Price – and perhaps Domino as well – was as yet a drop in the musical ocean, for the balladeers reigned and so, Stateside, did the country-and-western artists like Hank Williams and Kitty Wells. Wartime thoughts had not been forgotten, for the golden girl of World War II, Vera Lynn – 'The sweetheart of the forces' – together with Roland Shaw's orchestra and a chorus of soldiers, sailors and airmen of His Majesty's Forces scored the number-one spot both sides of the water with 'Auf Wiedersehn Sweetheart'.

Bennett's two million sellers of 1953 were 'Stranger in Paradise' (later to triumph in Britain) and 'Rags To Riches' with the latter penned by Adler and Rose who had also written the famous musicals *Damn Yankees* and *The Pyjama Game*. Also sharing some of the Stateside notice for 'Stranger in Paradise' were the Four Aces who, apart from selling into six figures with this number from the musical *Kismet*, had gold discs in the first part of the decade for 'Tell Me Why', 'Victoria', the Academy Award winning song of 1954, 'Three Coins in a Fountain', and the Academy's Best Film Song of 1955, 'Love Is A Many-Splendoured Thing'.

Tony was joined in the 1953 million-selling listings by Eddie Fisher's 'I'm Walking Behind You', Frankie Laine's most powerful 'I Believe' (which was to become Britain's all-time most number-one positioned disc) and four big hits from the mighty Fats Domino.

For Bennett and others of his kind this was to be the last year of comparative freedom and musical peace before the rock 'n rollers would come and snatch the young away. But while many cowed and slunk away into banishment and obscurity Bennett joined in the battle, and not believing the day of the singer or song was over, he continued on the success trail and indeed still attracted many young fans. Perhaps it was partly due to his technical brilliance as a performer, though at this period of his career he was still polishing his vocal technique and his act: maybe he owed his success to the warmth and depth of feeling which he displayed – whatever the cause he was to stay on the musical scene.

There could be another reason for his longevity: Bennett was too much into his own brand of popular music to worry about what was emanating from elsewhere.

'I never bothered too much about rock and roll. In the Fifties while Elvis was booming, the sound of the business started to change. I knew a lot of those guys would clean up but I still couldn't sing any of that stuff.

'I figured that there would always be a few people around who like to hear the good things, songs with lyrics that told a story. Young people, too.'

And Bennett – compared to some – invested himself in his music so much that second best was irrelevant as a consideration and his own pursuit of the first-rate meant that he kept his standards.

'It's important to me to make every record the best I can make it. Every record to me is like my own thumbprint or photograph. When it's finished I've got to live with it for the rest of my life.'

It was a philosophy of music and of life which would bring in rich dividends.

And he was governed by thoughts like: 'You have to aim at something that lies within your capacity. It's no use planning your entire life on the assumption that you are going to win a fortune from the football pools. You must set yourself a realistic objective. Once you have discovered what this might be, the sky's the limit.' So it was to prove for Bennett.

There was no further million seller for him Stateside until 1957 when he took a basic pop song with a twist, a lilt and an infectious title line called 'In the Middle of an Island' high up the charts. The interim period was filled with a number of moderately well-selling 45s, including Top 20 numbers 'Can You Find it in Your Heart', 'From the Candy Store on the Corner to the Chapel on the Hill' and 'The Autumn Waltz'. But if Bennett was silent on the 'gold' disc trail there was plenty of noise from Jerry Lee Lewis with 'A Whole Lotta Shakin' Goin' On'; magic from Buddy Holly and the Crickets with their captivating 'Peggy Sue': Presley hitting the heights with numbers like 'Jailhouse Rock', 'All Shook Up', 'Too Much', 'Teddy Bear' and 'Loving You' all combined for a fantastic era, and Tommy Sands from the US TV show *The Singin' Idol* had 'Teenage Crush'. Bill Justis found a million seller (his only one) with 'Raunchy'; the Crickets had 'That'll Be the Day' with Holly on lead vocal, and Johnnie Ray found a new lease of life with 'Just Walkin' In The Rain', which had formerly been recorded by The Prisonaires, inmates of the Tennessee State Prison.

But while Haley, Presley and the new breed made the running, Bennett was calmly collecting his royalties with none of the fuss and bother which attended the others. He was also turning into something of a vocal sensation in Britain. He became a household name in 1955 when his earlier US hit 'Stranger in Paradise' shot into the number-one position. Unlike some other 'newish' artists from across the Atlantic he was welcomed warmly by a country still reasonably free from the incursions of pop, a land where the 'good' song and the quality artist were always welcome.

When Bennett topped the UK charts on the week ending 28 May 1955, his rendition was one of three versions. The Four Aces for Brunswick were at nine and one place below was the HMV released version by Tony Martin. The three 'Strangers' were joined in that week's chart by two 'Cherry Pinks' and three 'Unchained Melodies' which chart mathematicians soon realized meant there were eight best-selling discs using only three tunes! Along with Bennett's 'Stranger in Paradise' the Brits of the time could also hear, among others, Ray's, 'If You Believe', Doris Day's 'Ready, Willing and Able', Lanza's 'I'll Walk With God', Jane Forman's 'I Wonder', 'Because of You' from Sammy Davis Jr and Sinatra with 'You My Love'.

And while 'Stranger in Paradise' continued to hold the top spot at the beginning of June it was announced that Rosemary Clooney would play the London Palladium for two weeks from 18 June, Dean Martin and Jerry Lewis were rehearsing songs from the duo's latest film *You're Never Too Young*, singers Teddy Johnson and Pearl Carr announced their wedding date and Danny Kaye was playing a limited season in London. But at this time pop was still only one facet of show-business. The *Record Mirror*, for instance, was a show-biz-cum-music paper and the day when thousands of words would be written on 'image' artists was far, far in the future.

The front page of the *Record Mirror* for the week ending 16 July was given over to Philips 'The Records of the Century' which, without mentioning any particular single or LP, merely said 'Greetings to Tony Bennett'. Two decades on, the advert would have said clearly what was at stake – for Bennett was in Britain for his first visit, with the week commencing 18 July to be spent at the Empire, Glasgow and that from 25 July at Liverpool's Empire. The *Record Mirror* ran a story of how Bennett had been signed for his two weeks' variety tour without impressario Mitch Mitchell having seen him.

'But he had heard him, and that was enough for Mitch. One listen to Tony's auditioning convinced Miller that the Bennett boy was the goods. How right he was. The twenty-eight-year-old singer proved his disc mastery again with "Cinnamon Sinners" and of course the fabulously successful well-in-the-top-ten "Stranger in Paradise".'

In one sense an air of unreality hangs over the extract, for was not Bennett an established US artist with several million-sellers to his credit? Well, yes, of course, but there was the Atlantic: there was a time gap between the two countries in the 1950s, and Britain had kept her distance.

Equally there might – to modern ears and eyes – be something strange in the fact that a major star should have such a short tour without even appearing in London: not that there was or is anything at all wrong with either Glasgow or Liverpool, but in show-biz the real acclaim lay in a season at the London Palladium, a booking and venue which added to an artist's international

80

standing. Gee Nicholl, the gossip columnist of the *Record Mirror*, seemed to feel this way when she wrote: 'I won't be surprised to see this vocalist coming back again for a season at the Palladium.'

But whatever the show-biz politics, Bennett had a great time on his first British visit. Philips threw a well-attended reception and were generous with the decor, food and drink. Bennett met other luminaries including Marlene Dietrich and in enthusiastic tones commented: 'She's so marvellous. Not only in her act but as a person. She told me all about Bessie Braddock too, and the visit to the House of Commons.' He was fascinated by London's historical sites and buildings: 'It's so wonderful. I'm spending every minute I have seeing places I've always wanted to see for years,' was his comment. He played some golf and indulged in a growing hobby of his – painting, (he owned a Japanese painting set and used the bamboo and sable brushes like a master).

He was also fascinated and captivated by a new Philips radiogram and told the pleased Philips people that there was nothing to touch its standard in the States. 'At home I've one whole room of my study taken up by a hi-fi set and I've got a speaker as big as this whole set but the sound's no better!'

He brought with him Chuck Wayne, alias Charles Jagelka, a thirty-two-year-old ace guitarist who had formerly been with the Woody Herman band and known to jazz buffs in that quarter for his soloing on 'Summer Sequence'. He had also been an original member of the George Shearing Quintet. It was interesting that Bennett brought a guitarist partner rather than a pianist with him, and a jazz man at that. Wayne had also his own trio for a short time and it included in its line-up Birmingham-born pianist Ronnie Ball. When Wayne had a resident group at a US night club Le Downbeat, the tenor was Zoot Sims, later to be associated with the great Stan Kenton and of course to find his own jazz acclaim.

Bennett's visit was arranged for a 'here today, gone tomorrow' finish. The last show was 31 August and he had a booking on the US East Coast in New Jersey on the first day of September. Bennett quipped, with some amusement, 'I'll be singing the last few lines as I step on board the plane!'

By the time he left, 'Stranger in Paradise' had fallen out of the British top ten but revenues are the same whether the top or flip side of a record is popular and it was not surprising to see 'Paradise's' other number, 'Take Me Back Again', given some sales impetus. Bennett told publishing man Bert Corri, the exploitation chief of Francis, Day and Hunter, 'It's one of the most successful of my career – a great number!'

And there was one other noteworthy happening for Bennett in London – it was here that he saw *Kismet* for the first time! Yet he had a million-selling US hit and a British chart-topper with 'Stranger in Paradise' from the musical! More than one observer quipped that it might be a good idea if all artistes who were recording a song from a stage show were to avoid seeing and hearing it sung in its original context!

Bennett returned to the States and left many fond memories and a bevy of fans committed to buying each and every release. 'Close Your Eyes' made the Top 20 but the autumn release of 'May I Never Love Again' coupled with 'Don't Tell Me Why' lacked either the exquisite melody line of 'Stranger in Paradise' or the happy love lyric. Both songs were well sung but they promised little in themselves and, sadly, this was reflected in poor sales.

Surprisingly, for all its chart-topping success, the UK release of 'Stranger in Paradise' was not in the Top Ten for the year 1955 as a whole. It came twelfth with 'Rose Marie' from Slim Whitman, Laine's 'Cool Water',

Tennessee Ernie Ford's 'Give Me Your Word' and Perez Prado's 'Cherry Pink' occupying the top four places.

Tony had just one more British hit left for the 1950s and obviously after the tour and record success of 1955 it was a disappointing state of affairs. Fortunately thirteen titles were to chart in the States by the end of the decade. The British hit, 'Come Next Spring' which came in 1956, also charted for him back home. The reviewer in *Record Mirror*, 14 January 1956, saw it as 'a delightful disc' and thought that on both the main side and its flip, 'Afraid of the Dark', Tony surpassed his vocals on 'Stranger in Paradise'. Late in April, UK Philips released 'Forget Her', coupled with 'Can You Find It in Your Heart?' The main side was a sentimental number while the other saw the singer in rocking vein, with a vocal back-up from an unnamed lady.

Among the thirteen US hits was a million-seller-plus – 'In the Middle of an Island' which was written by Nick Acquaviva and Ted Varnick. Unfortunately for Tony his thunder was stolen in Britain by a popular British group, The King Brothers, the disc being their second hit, 'Following a White Sports Coat'. It was typical of this decade in which UK artists watched like hawks to see what was happening across the waters. If they had the chance they would put out their own version of an American hit, a practice which, as in the case of 'In the Middle of an Island', could sometimes prove very remunerative even if otherwise disastrous for the poor artist who had recorded the original. But it was disappointing to see Tony's fine version buried. The gradual growth of sound and visual sources in the UK contributed greatly to this phenomenon with the home-grown musicians able to take advantage of the new expanding media opportunities.

Tony came back to Britain in 1958 for ATV's *Sunday Night at the London Palladium* and *Saturday Spectacular* but apart from generating expectant and ultimately satisfied audiences the visits did not occasion a massive rise in his general popularity. Early in the year Philips released 'Love Me Love Me Love Me', coupled with 'I Never Felt More Like Falling in Love'. As might be expected Bennett's vocal work came in for praise from the reviewers but no-one thought the songs strong enough to put him back into favour with record buyers. The main side was rather quiet and restrained, and this mood was maintained with the B-side, though 'I Never Felt More Like Falling in Love' did contain an attractive hook-line.

While this record was floated on the market, Presley was topping the British charts with 'Jailhouse Rock'; the rich vocal tones of Bing-Crosby-sounding Michael Holliday were capturing hearts and memories with 'The Story of My Life'; Sinatra was enjoying sales for 'All The Way', and Jimmie Rodgers from America engaged in battle with Frankie Vaughan's UK cover version of 'Kisses Sweeter than Wine'. Philips itself had issued 'Miss Me Just a Little' from Johnnie Ray and 'Put a Light in the Window' from The Four Lads; Mitch Miller was marching happily to his 'Theme from Bridge Over the River Kwai (Colonel Bogey)' and Britain's golden girl Anne Shelton was singing 'Ha! Ha! Ha!' with the emotive 'Until They Sail' on the flip. Back in the States, Tony continued his round of the big nightclubs and major TV shows. The visual network had proved influential and important in his career, after all he was among the first of the new bunch of artists who utilized the growing importance of television. And during the decade he starred in a five-week summer series on NBC and a special musical salute to George Gershwin.

Bennett recalled the early days: 'TV was so primitive in those days that the stage hands held up cue cards. Sometimes the words would be upside down. Rosemary Clooney and I would have to improvise right on camera.

Remember it was live in those days. Sometimes the words we made up turned out better than the amateur's lyrics.'

The decade closed with the release of the album *Hometown, My Town*, which was a musical portrait of New York City in its many moods, presented via extended performances of six songs. He began with a fine rendering of Gordon Jenkins' haunting 'Skyscraper Blues' and among other cuts were 'I Cover the Waterfront' and 'The Party's Over'. It had been a decade of big hits, near misses and failures. Tony Bennett had charmed and drawn huge crowds and shown that he could live quite well without having hit records though there was no doubting a big hit could bring him before a very wide audience. This was the case with 'Stranger in Paradise' which in Britain unfortunately proved an unrepeatable success where in the States there was also a huge sale for 'In the Middle of an Island'.

By the end of the 1950s Bennett had, to many people, become two persons – there was the sophisticated charmer of the albums and the more easy-going popular man of the singles. In the former persona he drew sales from those who willingly paid top prices to see him in the nightclubs. On vinyl some of his finest moments had come from the jazz flavoured LP *The Beat of My Heart*, which was recorded with some of the best instrumental soloists Stateside. Other choice albums were *Tony Bennett Showcase, Long Ago and Far Away, Tony Bennett in Person* (co-featuring the Count Basie Band) and *To My Wonderful One*. Bennett's excursions into jazz fields showed his growing quality and versatility and were musical miles away from his pop moods even if they were highly lucrative, with 'In the Middle of an Island' as good an example as any – a pleasant song but one which hardly stretched the man's vocal ability. By the time the 1960s were at their last breath, Tony Bennett was firmly nailed to a quality masthead. It no longer mattered whether he had hit singles or not, for he was above the rustlings of the pop business with its obsession with image and instant rapacity.

Bennett was sailing into 'all-time-great' territory, not so much by virtue of chart pre-eminence as because he was a singer's singer who fortunately also had an appreciative audience which was both wide and divergent. He was spoken of in the same breath as other great singers and entertainers and many of them paid him flattering compliments.

By the end of the 1960s he had become the establishment's musical son. He had played every place on the strip in Las Vegas. His concerts at the famed and legendary Carnegie Hall in New York were sold out well in advance. There was the same ticket mania when he played other great centres like Chicago's Empire Room and the Copacabana and the Waldorf in New York. When he toured England near the end of the decade people even said that he rivalled the Beatles – such was the stir his visit caused in some musical circles.

Bennett sang at the prestigious Royal Command Performance before Britain's Queen in 1966 and a year later he was a special guest at the White House where he displayed his vocal powers for the pleasure of President Lyndon Johnson and his guest, the prime minister of Japan. On March 3 1955 he stunned even senior members of the musical world by attracting 53,000 people to the Lincoln Center's Philharmonic Hall, an audience which was then a house record. He had bridged generation gaps. A new music had arrived in the 1950s called rock 'n roll and another came in the 1960s, headed by the Beatles and endless other British groups, to be followed by psychedelic rock and the blues revival which merged into a heavier musical sound; yet through all this Bennett had survived. It was something which *Record Mirror* noticed when they awarded him a special tribute supplement at the beginning of the next decade.

His biggest compliment came from the governor of popular music, Frank Sinatra. Frank awarded Tony Bennett the ultimate accolade when he called him 'the greatest singer in the *world*', and to the name of Sinatra in the Bennett fan stakes could be added those of Count Basie, Woody Herman, Louis Armstrong, Duke Ellington, Dizzy Gillespie, Buddy Rich and many more. Judy Garland said 'Tony Bennett is the finest male entertainer in the world today', while another fan, the famous US DJ and TV presenter-personality Ed Sullivan, said, 'He is the number-one singer in the world', and Fred Astaire, one of the greatest dancers, music-hall and film personalities of all time, declared: 'Tony Bennett is in a class by himself.' Buddy Rich called him 'a Picasso' and added, 'He's a Rembrandt and he's pop art – all at the same time.'

Dizzie Gillespie said 'Talking about Tony Bennett is the same as a finished musician playing a solo; you don't need twenty-five choruses to get your message across. I can tell you in a few words. I think Tony's spirituality is so profound in his performance that it cuts through everything superfluous, and what's left is raw soulfulness. Because his philosophy of life is so basic, the moment he opens his mouth to sing you know exactly what he is – a prince. I really feel that guy!'

Baritone saxophonist Gerry Mulligan commented, 'I like Tony – very much. Many times, I like people and I don't know why. But I know why I like Tony. He's an emotional singer; and without really wringing it out, he gets the feeling out of a song that's in it. And he's himself at all times; he sings *Tony*. That's exactly what better musicians try to do.' And Mulligan's fellow jazz giant Herbie Mann said: 'Anybody who can make hit records out of good music nowadays, has got to be an exceptional performer. In Tony's case, I appreciate the dimension that most other singers don't have. The third dimension: Truth.'

The Bennett concerts – certainly the big affairs – may have been in front of star-studded or silver-and-gold-bespangled audiences but at ordinary concerts he was heard by all sorts and shapes and sizes of humanity. And as *Record Mirror* astutely observed, here was an artist who broke the teenage generation barriers which the pop culture industry had largely assembled and preserved as their commercial bandwaggon. 'Teenage audiences respond to Tony's emotional delivery, his exciting rhythm. His swinging beat. Through the years young people have always been in the forefront of his fervent admirers.'

He was in London in 1961 and apart from his major purpose of starring at the Pigalle it gave him the chance to meet up with some British musical friends.

'Frankie Vaughan and his wife are two very good friends of mine. Frankie is a wonderful person to know and a first-class entertainer. The folks back home think he's swell, too.' And he soon came to realize that here on his second visit he was likely to be recognised: 'Even in three years or so London has changed. It's far more internationalized and the customs have become less formal and more relaxed. Once in a while people actually address me as "Tony" nowadays!

'My nose stops me being conceited, with my nose that would be an impossibility! I know it looks as though it has been stepped on by the Brigade of Guards. I've lost movie contracts because I've refused to be pressurized into an operation but it's my proboscis and it's going to stay the way it is!

'I tell you the girls in Britain are beautiful, beautiful, beautiful – and no other comment!'

His booking at the esteemed nightclub Pigalle was for four weeks starting 17 April 1961. The gap between then and his past series of concerts was eight years. But the artist realized that his visit this time had a major difference:

'When I came before I appeared in variety but then I found in 1961 that the music halls were a spent force in Britain and I'm prompted to voice my opinion that it's a terrible shame.' Not of course, an unfamiliar state of affairs in his experience for he, in common with musical troubadours, had seen the gradual demise of vaudeville until it had passed into American musical history. And seeing this happen he had switched his attention towards cabaret work and had by the end of the 1950s pencilled in more club dates than anything else. 'I would have loved to tour the theatres again, it would have been like old times but I enjoyed the Pigalle very much.'

One of these dates was the already mentioned one-man show at the Carnegie Hall in New York on 9 June 1962. The performance had been sold out two weeks in advance and almost two thousand fans were turned away after stage seats were filled. The programme, ranging through such US Bennett hits as 'Lullaby of Broadway', 'Stranger in Paradise', 'Firefly', 'How about You', 'April in Paris', 'Solitude', 'Always', 'Blue Velvet', 'Rags to Riches', 'Because of You', 'One for my Baby' and 'Sing You Sinners', brought the audience constantly to its feet. Though only his top hits were programmed it took two records to complete the recording. *Tony Bennett at Carnegie Hall* was issued in the USA in September 1962.

Tony returned to the Carnegie Hall on 23 November and treated his audience to a fare of more than forty different selections of material. A large orchestra that included strings, harps and vibes, as well as the expected reeds, brass and percussion, helped carry off his fine programme. There were a number of top-rated jazz musicians who were featured as soloists: Don Elliott on vibes; Al Cohn on tenor sax; Kenny Burrell on the guitar; and Ralph Sharon as conductor and pianist.

The audience was mostly aged between twenty-five and forty-five, and Bennett gave them numbers from the quality standard book; 'Old Black Magic' (featuring a superb Cohn solo), 'Chicago,' 'Fascinatin' Rhythm', 'Sing You Sinners', and so on. Old-time or soon-to-be-established Bennett numbers like 'I Left my Heart in San Francisco', 'Rags to Riches', 'Once upon a Time', 'Just in Time' and many others followed. There were some new numbers including three from the Sid Caesar hit 'Little Me'. Critic Jack Maher commented: 'All were done with a sense of theatre too, for each tune seemed to build to the close. Tony, like a crafty veteran pitcher in baseball, grew stronger as the night grew longer. His voice seemed to gain in dynamics and intensity as the programme moved toward its three encore close. Columbia Records did not record this concert, and it's a pity, for if they had, it would certainly have been a smash.'

'A certain amount of pomposity crept into the pop business in the sixties,' said Bennett. 'Just as the movies went Cinemascope, so the same thing happened to the length of concerts. I can listen to music all day long but the average layman has a certain appetite and after a certain time the boat sails. I learned this from the Paramount Theatre. It had the best variety shows possible – the Dorsey Band, Sinatra, people like that. And they never ran more than one hour fifteen minutes.

'I think if a show runs longer than that the audience starts worrying about the baby sitter and personal problems. As professional artists are starting to do more and more concerts I think they should come down to seventy-five minutes for a show – without an interval of course. I believe audiences like that.'

However there was the occasional concert Stateside, a dance or two, one of which had given rise to his LP with Count Basie *In Person*, which was recorded live. Basie was someone Bennett greatly admired and at the time in 1961 he said further recordings together would be most welcome. It seemed the obvious course of events since he spent several weeks a year touring with this exciting outfit.

'No kidding,' he said, of touring, 'those two weeks always turn out to be the most exciting, memorable and musical of the year for me.'

Bennett had survived the musical ravages of the rock 'n rollers of the previous decade and he was never too polite about the sound they made even from the vantage point of later time: 'There are good teenage records around. But I don't agree with the sense of juvenile delinquency which is reflected in some of the records.'

He told of a dearest dream of his that when he was next in a town where the Stones or Beatles were also billed then he would like to transport hundreds of kids in a fleet of buses from his concert to theirs and from that point to a classical auditorium for a recital by a Heifetz or a Horowitz or Segovia. His comment on the practical result of putting the dream into reality was: 'The kids of today know what's happening, and they'll recognize everything that's good in music – not just rock.'

And a few years later in the mid-1960s he said: 'But much of it is such mumbo-jumbo. I really believe too that the public prefers fine, quality music. They like people like Lena Horne, Johnny Mathis and Ella Fitzgerald. I'm not saying that the Rolling Stones should sing 'Stranger in Paradise', but the public has more taste than the record companies realize. I guess I'm old-fashioned. I think songs should be lovely illusionary things that take people's minds off their everyday problems.'

Unlike the stars from the Beatles period onwards, Bennett had to find songs and certainly early in his career there were few problems. The great shows and musicals supplied many fine numbers and songwriting was still regarded as the work of craftsmen – artists had not got to the stage where they realized that they could hum melodies and let someone else construct the song.

So as the 1960s progressed he was raking even more thoroughly through the Broadway shows of the 1920s and 1930s and 1940s for his recorded material. But, as previously mentioned, he was an initiator and not an imitator and he was always encouraging new writers and willing to make bold experiments. As he said: 'Good songwriters and lyricists are as sparse as a flower on a high mountain. I'd rather wait years for one fine musicianly piece than sing a mediocre number, and, believe me, there are thousands of those lying on the shelves of Tin Pan Alley.' In the opinion of many, Bennett almost single-handedly discovered bossa nova music in South America.

But there were good songs and there were good records with one of the most interesting – out of those which failed to chart – the UK-CBS release 'You'll Never Get Away from Me' coupled with 'Marry Young', which was released in the middle of November 1962. The top side came from the musical *Gypsy* and was sung in the original show by Ethel Merman and Jack Klugman. Tony was accompanied by his long-time accompanist, British-born Ralph Sharon, and he and his orchestra gave superb support in a version of the *Gypsy* 'hit' which, although different from the original, kept the fire and excitement.

For Bennett the 'great success song' of the decade was 'I Left my Heart in San Francisco', a song which could have been lost forever since it remained for a considerable time in cold storage. Written in 1954 by Douglas Cross and George Cory, it provided Tony's sixth million seller and had sold around two million copies by 1964. Sales have steadily increased since then and wherever Bennett sings the song is heard, so heavily has it become associated with him. His rendition was aptly rewarded by his winning the Grammy Awards Best Male Vocal Performance and Record of the Year in 1962.

'I recorded that song and it was so successful yet the

strange thing is I didn't actually see it as a hit. I sang it at the suggestion of my pianist, Ralph Sharon, during a show in San Francisco. It went down so well, I just had to record it and it just sort of snowballed. The way I look at it, a record is permanent. It's like a photograph or thumbprint. I've got to live with it for the rest of my life. When I first heard "Shadow of your Smile" I spent the whole of a summer trying to get it right then, suddenly, it clicked and I recorded it.' When it was first issued in Britain by Philips it caused little reaction but re-issued by CBS in March 1965 it sold 10,000 records in seven days at one point and was doubtless helped at the time by Tony's singing the number on the high rating Andy Williams show on BBC TV.

Later on, in the 1970s, Bennett and the city celebrated the record's success with a Tony Bennett day. The star drove in for the special occasion, left his car in an unauthorized spot and was given a parking ticket!

The America in which 'I Left my Heart in San Francisco' triumphed presented a mixed musical scene. There was a revival in the folk field, which had burgeoned through the popularity of artists like Flatt and Scruggs, Peter, Paul and Mary, the Chad Mitchell Trio and Joan Baez. Country had spilled over into folk with bluegrass performers and maintained its own identity. Pop people flocked to Nashville in an attempt to capture what was aptly, even if unimaginatively, called 'the Nashville sound'. Rhythm and blues continued to exercise a large influence, while there was a greater readiness to accept foreign material, surging and hot records, and – more potent in terms of Bennett's career – there was a revival of standards and the writing of what the industry termed 'good' songs. Nat 'King' Cole's 'Lazy, Hazy, Crazy Days of Summer' was one example, another was the revival of 'Deep Purple', and Tony's etching of 'San Francisco' fitted neatly into this scene.

Bennett's success with San Francisco saw the LP of the same name listed as the fifth best-seller in the *Billboard* listing of leading LPs – 1963. Ahead of *I Left my Heart in San Francisco* was *Joan Baez in Concert*, which was placed fourth with Peter, Paul and Mary's *Moving* a place above. The same trio occupied second place with an album simply entitled *Peter, Paul and Mary*, and at number one was the sound track of *West Side Story*.

In the American trade paper's listing of Top Singles Artists for 1963 Bennett was placed at 30, no mean feat for someone whose orientation was not basically directed towards AM radio and the pop market. The top five singles for 1963 were the Beach Boys, Dion DiMuci, The Four Seasons, Ray Charles and Chubby Checker. In terms of 'quality' artists there was only, apart from Ray Charles, Andy Williams at 15, Nat 'King' Cole at 20, Brook Benton at 26 and Al Martino at 27, ahead of Bennett. It should be said however that Tony was never a singles-orientated artist even if he did have singles hits. He himself says: 'Any time I can communicate it matters. Luckily I've had a consistent level.' But he was uninterested in the frenzied instant world of 45s where one disc follows another to keep hit momentum at peak and where many artists fall by the wayside.

He wanted hits – no doubt about that – but these would hopefully not come from the hype of pop promotion and would be sold on content and not the trappings. 'You see I can work all the time without them, but they increase my drawing power. I think I'm on my own in one respect in this business, though. You see, I don't have my own music publishing firm – I feel strongly about this. People in this business come up to me and say "Hey, you could make a fortune if you published the song as well." My answer is that I don't want that fortune, I want to concentrate on the music. My duty is to see that songs are performed well. I've always felt that singers should sing and music publishers should publish. I sift the material they offer me. It's worked all right so far with me, so why should I change it?'

To Tony in 1963 talk of 'beat' music meant Count Basie and his music – 'Basie has a beat, and I can't say I find it in everything they say has a beat. Music doesn't have to be loud to have a beat – there's such a thing as a subtle beat. But hits, well they can change your career and a string of them can change things quickly – I'm in demand for many TV shows, movies, and personal appearances from now (August 1963) to December.'

If he did not shine in the singles charts, Tony did rather better in the list of top LP artists of 1963, for he came sixth behind Peter, Paul and Mary, Andy Williams, Joan Baez, the Kingston Trio and Ray Charles. Others in the Top Ten were Johnny Mathis, Allan Sherman, Robert Goulet and Nat 'King' Cole. As for the world at large, of the top 78 recording artists some 53 were American, and in taking a compilation listing of 'pop' charts Bennett found himself at 70.

Billboard's 'Who's Who in Popular Music' for 1964 carried a discography of American chart-toppers between 1948 and 1963 and noted how the tenure of records holding the number-one position had shortened considerably since 1948; for example in 1948 only ten records shared the top spot, whereas in 1962 some twenty records reached this position. Bennett was listed three times for 'Because of You' and 'Cold Cold Heart' in 1951 and 'Rags to Riches' in 1953. All three of course were million sellers, as was 'Stranger in Paradise', a British number one. From Bennett's point of view, 1963 had been far superior to 1962. In 1962, part from re-signing with US Columbia Bennett had been voted tenth favourite male vocalist with DJs. He had also enjoyed success with the album *My Heart Sings*.

In 1964 Bennett – like all US artists – faced the sudden

might of Liverpool and an American music scene which went British, though the popular rise of the Beatles in the States lagged months behind their first tentative UK charting with the single 'Love Me Do'. In 1964, however, the Beatles had nineteen singles in the US Top 40. Bennett had become familiar with the Liverpool group the Beatles before most Americans. He had seen them in a smoky underground club in Cologne, Germany. McCartney had caught his attention. 'I knew he was sprinkled with stardust the moment I saw him walk on stage. You know, with some people in show business – a certain few stars – a magic shines through their every move, whether they're performing or not. Instinct tells you they're destined for the top of the heap. Aside from the drawing power of his personality Paul really makes it happen as a live performer. Performance and presentation count for everything in transforming a song into a work of art and making a star out of a singer. A good performer has the ability to become a true artist if he really puts his heart into it.'

Bennett saw the Beatles making genuine creative and progressive music and felt that at the end of the day they qualified as good musicians. He expressed this view many years after the passing of the first wave of Beatlemania, which seemed to have more to do with commercial bandwagons and selling than anything inherently musical. This appreciative attitude was something he very rarely felt for the new artists, though he did praise two American performers, Bobby Rydell and Chubby Checker. However he was a pragmatic person and realized that even if he didn't like some of the new music, it still sent the cash tills ringing and encouraged many more people to buy records.

But undoubtedly, whatever Bennett or anyone thought of the Beatles and the mass of UK groups who surged into US recording schedules, once the 'Fab Four' had opened

(Melody Maker)

Painting has always been an important element in Tony Bennett's life. (Melody Maker)

Tony meets up with two famous British musical figures of the fifties: Jack Payne and Shirley Ryan. (Melody Maker)

Tony with the great Louis Armstrong. (Melody Maker)

Tony launching himself with a new record label – Phillips. (Dezo Hoffmann)

Bennett gives the lowdown to a fan. (Melody Maker)

Famed British bandleader and promoter, Vic Lewis, with Tony Bennett.
(Dezo Hoffmann)
Tony Bennett with jazz fan Spike Milligan at rehearsals for the Royal Command
Performance in 1965. (Dezo Hoffmann)

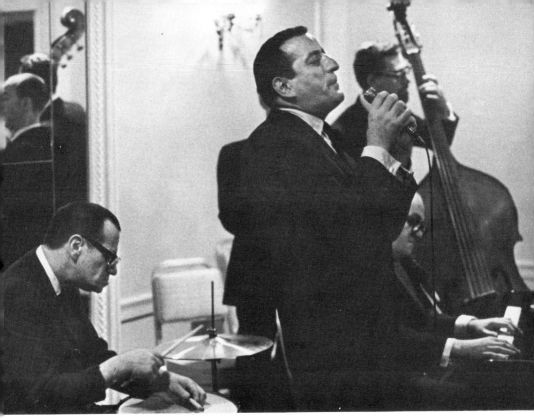

Performing at a press party at Claridges. (Dezo Hoffmann)

Signing autographs at Alex Strickland's Soho Record Centre. (Dezo Hoffmann)

Bennett has always sung with the best musicians of the jazz world. Here he is on stage with a member of Buddy Rich's band. (Melody Maker)

With Eric Dickson. (Hans Harzheim)

No passing strangers – with Billy Eckstine. (Melody Maker)

Taking a break with Count Basie's band. (London Features International)

And Tony has been around, for almost thirty years. (Dezo Hoffmann)

Tony with the Palladium's chorus line. (Melody Maker)

Two faces of the singer's singer. (Melody Maker)

(Melody Maker)

Tony with Minda Feliciano at a private view of his paintings in London. (Camera Press)

Tony with his wife Patricia. (Camera Press)

Revered doyen of the jazz critics, Max Jones, with Tony Bennett in 1982.
(Melody Maker)

(Melody Maker)

the floodgates, the effect was to lessen the chances of US quality artists finding record interest in their own country. The industry, seeing the fan-mania and the huge sums of money to be made, became progressively devoted to finding other teen sellers, though of course throughout Beatlemania/British mania, US heroes like Presley continued to hold their own as major-selling artists. Many record companies, however, had ceased to be much interested in the 'average' sale album from the so-called quality artist who could not be marketed and exploited in the same way as could the artist and groups who could fill the teen magazines with their pictures and gossip. Many quality artists themselves fell victim to the quick-and-easy buck philosophy and with it, though not entirely, went their own commitment to creating good music which would hopefully sell.

But for all the changing nature of the American hit parade, once the Beatles had first charted early in 1964 with 'I Want to Hold Your Hand', Bennett still sold albums and even in a declining musical world he filled halls. He explains his survival quite simply: 'In the day and age of the phenomenal Beatles, the rock 'n roll era and the so-called new modern music, it's funny how I find my own way by just doing my own thing. In choosing new songs I kinda go on my own instinct. I spend a lot of time each day looking at songs. I like to take the challenge of introducing new songs.'

Naturally he was asked why he did not record such and such a Beatle song. 'I was asked why I did not record "Yesterday" which was obviously a good song for me as opposed to some others. But when I sat down and thought about it, there were already twenty-five versions out. I liked the song very much and I would liked to have had the first "class" recording of it. I don't like that word "class" too much. I'm a pop singer. I sing popular songs.'

Among some of the things which happened early in the

1960s, apart from his visit to Britain, was Tony's appearance in a revival of *Guys and Dolls* in Chicago where he played the role of Sky Masterton. 'These shows – we call them "summer stock" productions back home – are important inasmuch as they provide a wonderful experience for someone like myself, who has his sights set on a Broadway appearance some time.'

His role in *Guys and Dolls* was his second taste of the stage because at the end of the 1950s he had appeared in a summer revival of *Silk Stockings* in Kansas City.

And early in the decade he eagerly followed developments concerned with a project of Sinatra's, the latter negotiating to buy the screen rights of the late Russ Columbo's biography and intending to cast Bennett in the film if the deal proved successful.

However Britain was a territory which he was increasingly concerned to conquer musically. In June 1964 he told Ray Coleman, *Melody Maker's* editor, that things were really looking up for him and would improve because he had made what he considered the best-ever record in his career, not withstanding 'San Francisco'. 'The song is "Danny Boy" and I was accompanied by Stan Getz and the pianist Hank Jones. Boy, that backing was so cool I was iced-up for the whole session.' As for the record's chances of making the charts he was less sure: 'Is it going to be a hit, I wonder? I know it will get played a lot by the radio stations but I think it may be a little jazzy for that hit business. Still, I enjoyed making the record more than anything I've done since "I Left my Heart in San Francisco".' He expressed the hope that he would return to Britain shortly and in 1965 this hope became reality. He made another visit to London's famed Pigalle, had a major British television programme, and played several provincial cities.

He played two concerts outside London in Manchester, but this meagre offering was scarcely enough to satisfy legions of Tony's fans, especially as for the many who reported and attended they proved one of the most memorable vocal experiences that British audiences had known for some years. Some 7,000 attended the London Hammersmith Theatre event and in untypical British – though very American – fashion, applause greeted each song as soon as it was recognized. There was much rapturous acclaim with 'I Left my Heart in San Francisco', and 'Who Can I Turn To' elicited the most cheers. The Johnny Spence Orchestra provided the musical accompaniments with Ralph Sharon conducting. The supporting trumpeter Bobby Hackett revealed much artistry; he particularly caught the ear for lead in 'It Had to Be You' and provided much beautiful musical colouring, especially to the ballads. For those who could not get seats the only compensation was the thought of seeing Tony in the summer TV schedules in *Burke's Law*.

In the various interviews he gave at the time he was keen to say what he observed about the new musical scene. He felt that many artists new to the music scene but equipped with a hit record were being thrown into situations with which they could not cope. It seemed part and parcel of the emergent music world that an artist with a hit record could guarantee a filled hall but all too frequently left dissatisfied fans who could plainly see that their newly acquired idol was unable to cope with the demands of performing a set and certainly had no idea what to do on stage.

'They get out on a stage to try and entertain somebody and they make fools of themselves. The most important rule for a young kid is: be a performer first and a record artist second. An artist today has to have individuality like, say, Hank Williams, who was the first to flash a gold cadillac with gold hubcaps. He started all that jazz, and Presley followed.'

Tony also stressed the importance of having good

management. 'Colonel Parker has done some job for Elvis.' And he urged aspiring young stars that they must never never stop studying and working towards their goal. He said they should take acting lessons and make use of every chance available to do film work, clubs, concerts and records.

As for himself and the Pigalle, he remarked with a wry smile: 'I first came to England seven years ago and I was pretty poor. Then I came back three years ago (1961) and I think I was a little better that time. Now that I've got another chance I'm very confident. I've had a lot of practice since the last time.' This sounds like modesty of the highest rank! But it reflects the feelings of an artist who knew he was star quality in his own country and yet was still very much seen as a new boy in Britain.

His television show was for BBC1 and was shown twice under the title of *Tony Bennett Sings*, the first showing was on 1 April and came under the general banner of *Show of the Week* and it was screened again on 18 November 1964. He presented some of his most successful numbers, including 'I Left my Heart in San Francisco', 'Who Can I Turn To?' and 'If I Ruled the World'. He was accompanied by his own rhythm musicians led by Ralph Sharon, thirteen of Britain's top session players and cornet star Bobby Hackett. Annie Ross made a guest appearance. The reviews were an artist's dream and included 'A Musical Treat', 'A first-class entertainer' and 'A singing star in every way'. Chronicler of big-band singers, author Ken Barnes, comments: 'It should be noted that Bennett is one of those rare singers who don't need the pianist to keep reminding them which key they're singing in. Once Bennett gets a note into his head, it stays there – regardless of interruptions.' He negotiated 50 per cent of the rights of the TV show for himself. 'Once I travelled with six managers in dark suits and an entourage. Now I've scrapped the management. I'm free. I saw Maurice

Chevalier walk through the back stage door once and decided I could learn something from him. Now I walk up to people and say I'm Tony Bennett. I'm here.'

At the time of the first transmission of his TV show, British CBS were publicizing his 'I Left my Heart in San Francisco' coupled with 'Candy Kisses' (which was in the charts at this period) and 'If I Ruled the World' with the poignant show song 'Who Can I Turn To?' from *Stop The World I Want to Get Off* on the flip. CBS announced on their Bennett posters that it was RISING FAST. The flip side was also the title of his new album.

Before the second showing CBS issued a special EP titled after Tony and containing four tracks: 'When Joanna Loved Me', 'This Is All I Ask', 'A Taste of Honey' and 'Fly Me to the Moon'. Accompanying artists on the prepared leaflet were Billie Joe Royal with 'I Knew You When', Winifred Atwell with 'Snow Bells' and Phil Tate's quickstep 'A Walk in the Black Forest'. It was a motley crew with differing musical styles.

And while he was in Britain he was pencilled in on Tuesday, 13 April, as star guest on the 100th edition of the BBC Light Programme series *Pop Inn*. Four days later, on the 17th, he was on the panel of *Juke Box Jury*.

He was also a VIP guest at a reception to launch the CBS British operation, then just a few months old. Goddard Lieberson, president of parent company Columbia, was present. US Columbia had formerly distributed its material through Philips, had briefly done business with Oriole, and was prevented from using its American company name because the word 'Columbia' was a copyright label of British-owned record company giant EMI Records. In November 1965 he sang at the London Palladium in the Royal Variety Show and this time, to accompany the attendant publicity, CBS released a beautifully delivered ballad 'The Second Time Around' coupled with 'The Shadow of Your Smile'.

101

Bennett arrived days after making a film called *The Oscar*, in which he played the part of a press agent and didn't sing a note: 'I really got starstruck,' was his smiling comment on that situation. He was cautious about committing himself to further films: 'Films can be a trap for a singer.' But as for singing to the Queen? Bennett regarded the event so highly that he stayed in London so that he could watch the show on TV.

'The show was one of my highspots, it had magic for me. The whole trip provided me with many memorable moments. Sharing a dressing room with Jack Benny, for instance. In America, he's an Old Master of show business and it was great thing to be working with him here. I took back many memories. It was a great honour. Quite overwhelming.'

Probably his sons Danny, nine, and Daegal, seven, appreciated another aspect of their father's visit. According to Tony at the time, 'They don't want to be a singer like me. They just want to be Beatles. Both boys have Beatle haircuts. One plays drums, the other guitar. And they call themselves The Dynamites. Can you beat it? I've got a personal mission and I accomplished it – I got the boys Beatles autographs.'

That autumn CBS in Britain issued *If I Ruled the World – Songs for the Jet Set*. It contained the title cut which had been a good-selling single, 'Song of the Jet' – a bossa hit from Brazil, Ellington's 'Love Scene', 'Fly Me to the Moon' and 'All My Tomorrows'. Arrangements were by Don Costa featuring the Ralph Sharon Trio and Al Cohn. The CBS press hand-out of the time, from their office at 104 New Bond Street, London, W1, quoted Frank Sinatra's comment in *Time* magazine: 'For my money, Tony Bennett is the best singer in the business, the best exponent of a song. He excites me when I watch him – he moves me. He's the singer who gets across what the composer has in mind, and probably a little more.'

At the end of 1965, international broadcasting company Radio Luxembourg announced 'that maestro of the smooth romantic ballad, Tony Bennett will soon have his own programme on Radio Luxembourg'.

Luxembourg radio people told how during his UK visit for the Royal Variety Show the singer had spent a considerable time at their Hertford Street studios in London and the result was a series entitled *The Many Moods of Tony Bennett*. The first show was scheduled for Saturday, 1 January 1966 at 8.15pm. It was to last for fifteen minutes and a thirteen-week series was envisaged.

Radio Luxembourg's press officer Barbara Hayes commented 'The show is all Tony's. A dynamic perfectionist, he is both compere and featured artist. We can guarantee that this will be a really great programme for all our listeners – whatever their age.' Another big event was to take place on home territory, for on 20 January 1966 Tony had his opening night at the famed Copacabana Club.

One reviewer remarked how the singer should have been thanked by the audience for agreeing to do a two-week stand, commenting on his skill and on the modesty with which between songs, he would thank someone in the audience – for example, Joe Levine, producer of *The Oscar* in which Tony had made his film debut, or Bill Gallagher, vice-president of Columbia Records (CBS-UK) – for 'comin' by'.

Bennett had a fifty-five-minute set that covered twenty numbers and was delivered with consummate skill in balancing rhythmic numbers, ballads, new songs and standards. He exercised complete control of his material and the audience sat enraptured. The songs on this occasion included numbers on which he had already stamped his trademark like 'I Left my Heart in San Francisco', 'Because of You', 'Who Can I Turn To', his current US disc of the time 'The Shadow Of Your Smile',

103

and standards 'Always', 'In My Solitude' and 'Taking a Chance on Love'. He also presented his next single 'Dream Your Dreams' for the Broadway musical, *Sweet Charity*, and the title number from the film *The Oscar*. He rounded off his set with 'The Trolley Song'.

While he triumphed in home territory in Britain there was much discussion in the music press over the so-called yoyo behaviour of his famous 'I Left my Heart in San Francisco'. *Melody Maker* recalled how the disc had first made its appearance in 1962 and how, because of the record's success he had been given the key to Golden Gate city on 9 July 1962. But following the song's US success and UK release had come several outbreaks of British buying with the record recharting in the winter of 1965; it had even outlasted the recent UK hit 'If I Ruled the World'. The exploitation manager at CBS, Roger Easterby remarked how a version by Fats Domino had perhaps reminded people of Tony's record so that they went out and bought his instead. The record was charting through Christmas 1965 and was at 23 in *Melody Maker's* first chart of 1966.

On 3 June 1966, CBS issued a ballad 'The Second Time Around' coupled with 'The Shadow of Your Smile' but it meant little. However, the next year, 1967, would herald some big things for the British – Bennett was booked with Count Basie to tour the country!

Before the vist BBC2 screened a repeat of his own *Show of the Week* which among other things had guest artist Annie Ross duetting with him on 'The Good Life'. The song, written by David Ross, came from the newly released film *Hombre*. Bennett performed it in superlative fashion. The flip side was an old Al Jolson song 'Keep Smiling at Trouble' which Bennett had performed on the Eamonn Andrews show during his visit the previous year.

CBS remarked 'Bennett's continuing popularity – he is

currently on a capacity booked tour of Britain with Count Basie – could be explained by the fact that he is his own severest critic. He will only record a song he feels is right for him and he insists on keeping in contact with the public through concert appearances.' They quoted Tony as saying, 'You get to know more about people by appearing in front of them, not by sitting in a recording studio or an office.'

Bennett was of course by now a recognized and frequent visitor to British shores and, as journalist Stan Reed told his readers, 'the excitement never palls'. It was certainly true in Manchester where the Free Trade Hall audience gave him such a reception that afterwards he found it difficult to put his feelings into words. Later he described the audience as 'fantastic – have you ever heard anything like it? I confess I'm used to applause but this was different – for the first few minutes on stage I hardly knew what to do. It seemed to be all-embracing – I've never experienced anything quite like that!'

Obviously for British fans there had been the initial Basie–Bennett interest and they were thrilled with what they heard. Of his collaboration with the famous bandleader and his musicians, Bennett commented, 'They are so creative. It's difficult to explain. I've been working off and on for ten years or so but this has been the first time since last summer. Just now they are reading a lot of parts! But wait till they get to know the parts. Then they put them away and the jazz really comes out.'

Basie was particularly pleased that famous player Earle Warren had been in the Basie line-up, for he remembered that Earle had been in his band when he had played his first nightclub now many years ago. He recalled how he had been so nervous in those times and he remembered with gratefulness how helpful Warren had been. Music writer Jerry Dawson told how he asked Bennett whether he preferred to vocalize with Basie or Ellington. Tony's reply was to be expected, for most singers of the Bennett mould would give half their savings or more to sing with either.

'I have no preference – just so long as it's good! I agree with Duke who has often been heard to say that there are only two kinds of music – good and bad. I don't mind what my backing is – trio, big band, orchestra – just so long as it is good.' He recalled his good fortune at having sung with Woody Herman, Stan Keaton, Duke and others: 'They are all great. But Basie himself always seems to enjoy every minute of what he's doing and this communicates to the band – and to me.'

As well as touring Bennett recorded an *In Concert* radio programme with Robert Farnon to be broadcast on 24 May and he had hopes of doing some television with Farnon. 'He's just the greatest conductor of them all. I first met him fifteen years ago and it has taken us all this time to get together.' He remarked with a smile that he had met Bob in New Jersey, USA, and now the conductor was living in Jersey off the British mainland. In fact he recorded material for several programmes, guesting in two Farnon shows and then appearing in *Be My Guest* where, in conversation with Harry Rogers, he talked about his early career – how he was spotted by Bob Hope, and sang in one of his shows and of the people he met on the way up, their music and their songs. Among the favourite artists he featured were Basie, Sinatra and Nat 'King' Cole.

And of course no visit can take place without some form of 'award' ceremony to spur on the endeavours of record-company employees and to gain some more column inches from the journalists. This time when he arrived for his tour he was to find not only the expected reception committee of well-known band leader and promoter Vic Lewis, agents Harold Davidson and Tito Burns and Roy Burns of song-publishers Campbell

Connelly, but an entourage from CBS who gave him a silver disc for a quarter million sales of 'I Left my Heart in San Francisco'. Pete Murray, DJ and TV presenter made the presentation. To tie in with his British visit CBS announced that they were releasing a new single entitled 'Days of Love'.

Once the British visit was out of the way Tony went to Europe for six weeks and then in July he booked in for three weeks at Sahara Tahoe. This was followed by two weeks at Las Vegas: all musical bookings were with Count Basie. The European tour included Paris and then to his joy a one-man concert in Rome. 'I couldn't wait to get there. Believe it or not I had never been there and I wanted to visit my father's birthplace. He was born in Calabria in Southern Italy (my mother was American-born of Italian parents) and I suppose I must have had a number of relatives there. It was funny really that I hadn't travelled abroad that much. Since 1962 when San Francisco really made me I'd been kept busy with every kind of show in the States – clubs, concerts, lounges and of course radio and TV.'

In December CBS had another Bennett single at the ready – 'For Once in My Life' coupled with 'How Do You Say Auf Wiedersein'. The main track was a lush ballad, faultlessly performed, superbly backed, which had all the signs of emulating even 'San Francisco'. CBS manager of press publicity, Rodney Burbeck said: 'Quality without gimmicks has always been the Tony Bennett stock-in-trade. Bennett refuses to bring himself into line with currently fashionable sounds or styles, preferring to forge ahead making records that involve him emotionally, with superior musicians and technical perfection.'

During this period Tony contracted his name to be used for 1,600 Spaghetti Houses ('Everyone in America knows I'm Italian') which would soon be found across the States. It was reported he would make a million from this. 'It's very alien to me because anything I have done in my life I've worked for. But yeah, I believe in money. I've lived without it and I've lived with it; it's just about the same, but it makes things easier.' However there was a curious rider to the statement: 'It doesn't appeal to me, it just appeals to all my relatives and friends – and Uncle Sam – and I get into an awful lot of trouble when I don't make it.'

And even money could not save the singer from one incident which happened in his room at the Dorchester. He was showing an electrician in which corner of the room he wished to have a record player placed. As he bent down there was a sound of tearing which sent him scuttling to another room. 'New,' he said on his return, face flushed and wearing a rueful expression. 'The first time I wear them and they split.' Even the most exclusive of tailors in New York had failed him.

Tony was back in Britain again before the decade ended, this time with ace-drummer and bandleader Buddy Rich, and within hours of arriving on a mild March afternoon the suntanned and smiling singer was swinging down at London's famous club Ronnie Scott's giving an impromptu performance with Buddy. It set the pace for a tour which also took Tony to Manchester, Leeds and Glasgow.

As he flew out of London at the end of the tour CBS issued a new single 'A Fool of Fools' coupling his voice with big-band backing. The flip 'The Glory of Love' had Tony duetting with his San Francisco buddy Dominic Germano. The song featured in the film *Guess Who's Coming to Dinner* and was given a breezy performance. Tony commented: 'Dominic is a great friend and a brilliant scat singer.'

Tony came to Europe for his next UK release 'Yesterday I Heard the Rain' – to be exact he located the song in Spain under the title of 'Esta Tarde Vi Llover'. The artist's soaring voice formed the perfect complement to this strong ballad. On the flip he paid tribute to the UK's Georgie Fame on a swinging arrangement of the Blossom Dearie song 'Sweet Georgie Fame'.

Another of his singles came from the film *Chitty Chitty Bang Bang* starring Dick Van Dyke, which was based on Ian Fleming's fantasy novel of the same name and opened with a bang in London. 'Hi Ho' had 'Hushabye Mountain' on the flip, the first single version of the title track from *Hushabye Mountain* and a ballad that brought him much acclaim Stateside.

The show *Funny Girl* had provided Barbra Streisand with 'People', which reached number-six in the US charts in 1964. It was taken up by soulsters The Tymes who had begun their days in 1959 and had been heralds of the sweet soul boom of the 1960s. Stateside the group took the song to 39 while in the UK it reached 16 early in 1969. It was the second of their five hits both sides of the water, the first being 'So Much in Love'. The Bennett class recording came in March 1969 – an impeccable recording combining Tony's tremendous vocal artistry with the Jules Styne/Bob Merrill composition. The flip was 'They All Laughed'.

The single 'People' released on 21 March preceded another UK tour which ran during the third week of April and saw the singer performing in London, Leicester, Bristol and Manchester. He told the press 'How does a singer get a good performance out himself? Through dedication to his own talent? Through his wish to communicate with the listener in the audience? Through the songs he personally believes in? In my own case I look at hundreds of songs before I choose one. When the song is right for me, I know it immediately. Naturally not every song can be a winner. But every song must be picked carefully; I've got to love it before I sing or record it.'

Bennett came with the Basie band once more and into

his concert repertoire he introduced a new song at the Free Trade Hall Manchester. The audience was privileged to hear the top-side of his latest single 'Play It Again, Sam', which had just been issued in America. About this song Tony says: 'It's a really good song. It's on the lines of "One for My Baby" and it's the title song from the Broadway show which was written by Woody Allen, who also stars in it.' Tony's recording of the song was used during the on-stage performance and planned for the film version. Needless to say the artist displayed impeccable phrasing and had the sensitive support of Torrie Zito's arrangement – with some superb trumpet fill-ins by Marky Markonvitz. 'Play It Again, Sam' was coupled with 'What the World Needs Now Is Love'.

There was more before the decade ended, with CBS issuing the single 'I've Gotta Be Me' which had a swinging big band sound. The number came from the musical show *Golden Rainbow.* Torrie Zito supplied a punchy brass section. The flip was 'A Lonely Place' from the motion picture *Heaven with a Gun.* Tony completed a cross-America tour, working with such top names as Buddy Rich, Woody Herman and Duke Ellington before the decade ended and enhanced his standing as one of the most appreciated entertainers in the popular music world of the day. Whether it was in a swinging, up-tempo or romantic melody mood, his warm, resonant voice and distinctive style had enabled him to survive.

So Tony Bennett had spanned another decade and indeed in the 1960s he had found fresh life, regardless of the changing forces of general pop music which by the end of the decade had gravitated into a whole host of new bands and singers on both West and East Coasts. The San Francisco and New York musical worlds had undergone a dramatic change of musical face at the end of the decade but Bennett the vocal maestro, remained impervious: as they say 'quality' generally wins through.

6.

Into the 1970s

THE RECURRENT STORY-LINE of Tony Bennett's musical career is the man's survival in an ever-changing musical world where scant respect is shown to the past or to the veterans of other decades and their stylization.

He came into the world of the 1970s with the knowledge that he had seen off the rock 'n rollers of the 1950s, whereas the likes of Larry Williams and Charlie Gracie had excited and found themselves rock 'n roll following but had faded. The following decade Bennett and fellow Americans had had to face the British invasion and the West Coast explosion, to name just two movements of the time; while numerous new names competed for prominence he and a handful of other troubadours continued to sing for their supper – and to win. The dawn of the 1970s promised much that was new but like any decade this one carried remnants of the past. Beatle magic had lost its main thrust but would continue thanks to material awaiting release, while the individual Beatles would create their own material and to some extent gain attention simply because they were and always would be seen as ex-Beatles, even after McCartney, for example, had founded Wings. The blues and rock people of the late 1960s would either get heavier, as with Deep Purple, or fade to see younger bands emerge with a more developed form of their sound. Some major bands and artists of the 1960s like the Stones, David Bowie and Eric Burdon (ex-Animals) would retain popularity.

In America the new musical forces calling for attention included Chicago Transit Authority and Santana, both bands displaying how you didn't have to be British to win national attention. UK band, Free, found popularity on both sides of the water, while British Joe Cocker, took his first steps towards his eventual legendary status with a Beatle song 'With a Little Help from My Friends'. Rock leadership lay with Led Zeppelin and from the vaults of the past but sounding as contemporary as anyone there came Tony Orlando. The industry in America still gave rock rather scant respect and there was a constant call for soft rock and even ballad singers. Of the latter, one eligible candidate who came to the fore early on was David Gates who fronted Bread. This group charted ten times in the US Top Forty between 1970 and 1972, and titles included 'Make It with You', 'If', 'Baby I'm A-Wanting You' and in a similar mould to the others, slow and emotive, 'Everything I Own'. Gates and Bread suggested indirectly that quality music could still make an impact. Indeed the 'song' came back in force as a number of female singers wrote and sang about their own experiences: their names included Dory Previn, Carly Simon, Joni Mitchell, Carole King and Anne Murray.

And of course there was the tail end of the Simon and Garfunkel success story. Their most popular number, 'Bridge over Troubled Water', was saved for 1970 release. Soon Simon began a solo career and showed clearly how a well-written song could still chart high and fetch high sales. Elton John, Aretha Franklin, a host of new black singers including teen sensations The Jackson 5 (otherwise known as the J5) and James Taylor would be among others vying for attention.

The beginning of the decade augured well for Bennett who had by and large kept himself away from some of the musical diversions of other quality artists, many of whom had made cover versions of songs which had been brought

112

to popularity by younger artists, sometimes from different musical genres. Certainly it's always been a favourite pastime amongst rather older pop singers to sing the current pop charts with the overall arrangement toned down from the original and given a greater degree of acceptability, especially if the hit artist has the image and lifestyle of an alien generation. And the practice has been more favoured in America than in Britain. Many American music lovers expect their artists to sing the hits of the day. Andy Williams and Johnny Mathis among others have done this from time to time, though the motivation tends to come from the record company headquarters, with the artists showing some hesitation.

But while record sources may have had designs on a charting Bennett in the 1970s, in the event this was to prove a decade without any Stateside Top 100 hit placing and the same was true for the UK Top 50. Yet of course by now he had long risen above the demands of so-called chart life and consequent pop publicity. He belonged firmly to a world where the passing whims and fancies of popular music were irrelevant. He had transcended the possibility of 'ups' and 'downs' as dictated by radio stations, TV corporations and writers, DJs and others who sometimes offer informed comment. He was becoming an institution; Tony Bennett was as much an American symbol as Coca Cola, or Macdonald hamburgers, blueberry pie or the stars and stripes. He could fill the big show-places without worry, and appeared on special occasions, along with other American 'greats' like Sinatra, Como, Dean Martin, Mathis or Williams. By now he had established a regular routine of international tours, giving a handful of concerts in major halls and clubs, complementing these with radio and television appearances.

Among the great moments for the artist who seemingly had been everywhere both physically and musically was his invitation from the London Philharmonic Orchestra in

1971 to sing with them at the famed Royal Albert Hall, in London. The orchestra consisted of ninety musicians including sixty strings. Bennett, from the confines of a plush London hotel, the Dorchester, commented: 'I am very elated as I have never performed with such an orchestra before.' Bennett's long-time aide Robert Farnon flew in from his Guernsey Hotel to conduct. The pianist was his own personal musical associate and accompanist, John Bunch. Bennett, who received a ten-minute standing ovation, was featured in the show's second half, the first being devoted to Scottish works.

It was a momentous beginning to the decade and the event was televised by BBC2 who waited for almost a year, to January 1972, before they showed the recording to the nation. Six and a half thousand avid fans were caught by the camera as it panned the great and impressive hall. Tony sang sixteen of his own special songs, including 'Country Girl', 'I Want to Be Happy', 'Let There Be Love', 'Love Story', 'There Will Never Be Another You', 'Wave', 'For Once in My Life', 'What the World Needs Now', 'I'll Begin Again' and of course 'I Left my Heart in San Francisco'.

This was one of a number of pleasant happenings in Britain for the artist and such was his delight at being in the old country that when he filmed a series for independent television he set up camp for three months. As a result, he found himself with free time, and so there came the desire to take up oil painting, now such a central part of his life. And from the early years of the decade during which he had spent so much time in the UK he recalls an incident which brought him much pleasure. He was sitting in his car in the West End of London, waiting for a friend: 'A crowd of girls, who I later learned were from a London choral school, recognized me. They lined up by a lamp-post and sang "San Francisco" all the way through. I know it sounds like a scene from a Hollywood

114

movie. But it's absolutely true – and you can imagine how deeply moved I felt.'

Bennett's love for British people was often expressed. 'They're so considerate of one another. They help people out. Some old woman down the road living alone. They'll all take turns in the neighbourhood stopping by and saying, "How are you doing mom? Is there anything you need?" They don't do it at home. They end up feeling better as a result of helping someone out.

'This is what I'm trying to say. I'm not coming on like a teacher because I'm not a teacher. Just from travelling around the world I've learned America is the greatest place in the world, but I think we have a lot of growing up to do. I think when we see something good in another country we should adopt it because it does work. Like, for instance, with less money than we have you've cleaned up pollution in London. People have actually raked out the Thames River. The people helped, the companies helped. Everybody pitched in and just cleaned it out. Now for the first time in five hundred years there are salmon swimming right in the Thames River. So they really help one another and it makes it a better place to live. We should pick up on things like that. It would be good for us.'

All this might appear to be a far cry from music, yet it is not quite so, for the atmosphere of Britain gave him the impetus to return again and again, and this extended into his television work.

'It's great working with British TV people. Some producer doesn't say "we'll do a country song" or "Take that song out" – things like that. They leave you alone. They respect the artist. They don't do things like that. They do beautiful light entertainment shows with Duke Ellington or Count Basie. In this country (America) if you see the musicians on television they only do one number, whereas there (UK) they do a whole hour.'

Bennett recorded thirteen television shows in 1972 and eventually they were put together and formed six specials. One was with Billy Eckstine, while others were with Matt Monro, Cleo Laine and Robert Farnon and his fifty-piece orchestra. The shows were recorded at London's well-known supper-club Talk of the Town: 'It was a beautiful club and I had a great time doing it.' There was one amusing tale from the series as Derek Witt recalls: 'It was recorded over a period of time. The tables had champagne bottles so people would know it was a club. However the boys went crazy for it was bogus champagne. But we had the real stuff.'

The specials, which were recorded in spring 1972, saw Bennett as both host and singer: 'You know in America all they've been able to afford is a seven-piece band for television. I think a full-scale orchestra is important.' For the Thames TV recordings Bennett got a 45-piece orchestra. He added: 'Music is international. I deliberately steered away from dialogue and patter at this time because I think it can get in the way of the music. I think it will be the first series in the history of television,' he added, 'that will never have a cue card. It's all been performed. In other words, the material is familiar to us. What I'm attempting, what I'm hoping for is something like what happened on the Billie Holiday recordings, where her songs were so believable because she lived them. In the same way, for twenty years I've been honing certain performances and now we're just putting them on film. They're things that have been proven to the audience, and I know where they lay and what the audience likes about them. They're not just something I just read off a cue card. They're songs that I've memorized and learned how to perform.

'My accompanist and fellow-artists are all hand-picked, all hand-chosen and they will also be doing songs without cue cards, doing their own songs. And we've rehearsed a duet which will be memorized throughout the week so there'll be a very healthy kind of workmanship every week. You know everybody will be working with something fresh and vital also.' And his guests were of the highest stature: 'Like Sarah Vaughan, she's the best singer around. And other old friends like Annie Ross, Billy Eckstine and Tommy Leonetti, and of course Cleo Laine and Matt Monro and Sacha Distel. Then there's the rhythm section: John Bunch, my musical director on piano, Arthur Watts on bass and Kenny Clare, drums. They're good musicians every one, and they'll stay with me for my tour as well.

'So this is a joy for me. Well, so long as John Bunch is playing piano, I'm happy. And Kenny Clare, he's magnificent. I'd play with Kenny any place in the world. As for Robert Farnon, who conducts the television orchestra, he's known as the guv'nor to all the top arrangers in America. He's so creative, such a sense of melody. Naturally I'm happy to be with him again. Like I talked about already, it's all going towards that good music I'm looking for. And so much depends on the conductor. As Bobby Hackett said: "If the conductor knows what he's doing, the show's relaxed, everything goes right."

'So you can see that we have the real pros on this TV series. And without standing on a soapbox I feel we kind of hit into the age of the amateur.'

Bennett didn't feel he was chancing his arm by choosing the guests on his TV series from the mainstream world of popular song. 'There are good singers that cannot be replaced, singers like the Sarah Vaughans and Billy Eckstines. I'm basing my show on the advice of Woody's (Herman) to go towards good music. And I'm keeping my fingers crossed on that. I go against what the advertisers say. I sing Gershwin, Rodgers and Hart, Vincent Youmans, also brand-new Cy Coleman songs that are very off-beat, some Bert Bacharachs and so on. And I find that the places wherever I play are filled up, so somebody likes it.'

He recalled some advice from Woody Herman: 'Just go toward good music,' aware that adopting such policy would entail conflict with some producers who failed to recognize the importance of setting high standards. 'He gave me the best tip I ever got from anybody. It's funny but I think I was already doing that. But it's like Pablo Casals told me one time: at any given moment you can learn. And that really is the best premise, because I find personally that when I sing a good song, that's when I feel best. I feel like I have something going for me, and there's some hope. It's when a producer comes along and says: "You're not singing the right song so we want you to do this" that I'm forced to sing something I really don't like. Then I become very upset. So unlike many other singers perhaps, it is difficult for me to sing anything other than what I feel really makes it – not only for the audience but for myself. I have to like it.'

But, of course, Bennett had by now virtually eliminated the problems of interference and had control of his own situation.

To Tony then in 1972 (and indeed, he has repeated this view on numerous occasions) there was no correlation between 'art' and 'dates' or 'fashion' and to illustrate this thought in tangible and practical form to jazz writer Max Jones he played Art Tatum's version of 'Willow Weep For Me'. His major British TV recordings would therefore represent quality and class.

His arrival for the 1970 TV series was preceded by news of his second marriage to former actress Sandra Grant and though this was doubtless unintentional it gave a good fillip to coming events. Although the two had lived together for seven years the actual marital vows and ceremony were seen as important and obviously the

118

singer's happiness was reflected in his music. He said just before the TV recordings: 'For the first time in my life I feel settled.' But as an earlier chapter has outlined the marriage was not to last.

Apart from his LPO concert and major TV commitments the decade had opened rather like the previous one, with a series of record releases sometimes related to touring or other media activity though in chart terms none of these songs was ultimately successful. On 20 October 1970 British CBS issued Bennett's recordings of 'MacArthur Park' and 'Eleanor Rigby'. The first from the hands of Jim Webb had already been a major chart triumph for actor Richard Harris with his version seemingly eating its way into the systems of countless adoring female fans. But the Bennett version was sufficiently different with his vocal brushstrokes making the song stirringly visual. Performance and presentation were again on a high level and the song became a new work of art. As the CBS press-officer of the time, Mike O'Mahony, said: 'Whether Tony Bennett is singing a swinging up-tempo number or a romantic melody his warm, resonant voice is able to create an aura around the song.' The flip saw the 1966 Beatles song given an interpretation which showed an empathy with the haunting nature of the tune. The release coincided with his series of dates at the London Palladium which commenced on 26 October.

By November, CBS UK had moved onwards with another release from Tony, this time in response to a definite public demand. It had been occasioned by the Palladium dates and his singing on the first night of the Leslie Bricusse composition 'I'll Begin Again'. The audience gave it a rapturous reception as though it were the first gem from a new star, whose promise gave people the impression that they were in at the start of a great career. The song came from the Cinema Centre film

119

Scrooge. It well illustrated, both in its original context and later on vinyl, how any singer can cut a record but only a star can make it happen in live performance. It was the perfect demonstration of the statement that performance and presentation count for everything in transforming a song into a work of art and making a star out of a singer; as Bennett once said: 'A good performer has the ability to become a true artist if he really puts his heart into it.' 'My Cherie Amour' appeared on the other side. For all its popularity the record failed to show up in the British Top 50, though perhaps its exclusion showed the failure of the chart system to pick up record sales from non-teenage-orientated record outlets.

But in many respects it didn't really matter for his overall popularity was assured. It was exemplified when – following thousands of letters that were sent to his manager, the BBC and Thames Television from dis-appointed people who were unable to get tickets for the singer's concert appearance at the Royal Festival Hall – he had agreed to play two special Sunday-night concerts at the Palladium on the evening of Sunday, 26 March.

When tickets went on sale for the Festival Hall concert on Saturday, 19 February 1972, the box-office was sold out within thirty-five minutes of opening; at that time an all-time record for the hall. Bennett was accompanied by a thirty-two-piece orchestra led by his musical director John Bunch and he stayed over in Britain another week so that he could appear in this extra concert. The RFH booking had followed concerts at the Guildhall, Portsmouth and the Birmingham Theatre, with two houses at both venues.

But there was no Basie this time. The 'Count' had recently opened at the St Regis Hotel in New York. Bennett said he had phoned the great jazz man and Basie exclaimed: 'What you doing in Europe without me?' Bennett added that the other purpose of his call was for him to say over the speakers at Basie's opening night, 'Here is Tony Bennett from London, England, and I may have left my heart in San Francisco but my heart's right with Count Basie tonight on his opening.'

Nor was Bobby Hackett with him. Bennett told Max Jones of *Melody Maker* that he thought Hackett was helping out the Kennedys a little; he had his own club and was still producing. 'Funnily enough, Bobby is still the most played artist in America. He has a very eccentric kind of career, because guys like us listen and just can't believe the music he's playing and yet they never announce his name. Yet if an FM station wants to get on the map, a quality station, every third record will be Hackett.'

Bennett mentioned that his new album, for release the summer of 1972, *The Summer of 42*, based on a movie theme, had Bobby playing a song. 'Bobby gets a beautiful, different quality.'

Bennett also mentioned his plans to record in Britain with the Bunch–Clare–Watts rhythm section. 'It will be my second trio album, and these take a lot more work because they're all involvement, you know. Of course, we have three months to kick it around. Then we're preparing a tribute to Duke Ellington which will be recorded here with Farnon and the orchestra. It will consist of Ellington songs, with Billy Strayhorn of course, and include some that are a little off-beat, like "Day Dream" and we're doing "Something To Live For" – I love that song.'

These record releases at the beginning of the decade were to be the last real attempt to sell Tony on a general popular level, and indeed early in the 1970s his record association with US Columbia, which had spanned so many years, was suffering badly. Eventually it came to an end and what seemed an ideal marriage of company and artist was left in disarray.

In October 1972, British Phonogram, part of the giant Dutch organization Philips, announced that they were delighted to have signed international artist Tony Bennett, with a contract covering the world outside the US (where he would be represented by MGM), Canada and Japan. Phonogram said the signing was considered a highly prestigious act and was the first to be negotiated with an artist of this stature since Steve Gottlieb and Roland Rennie became chairman and creative director, respectively, of Phonogram, London. The first release under this new umbrella was set for 24 November with an album called *The Good Things in Life* (Philips 6308 134, then retailing at £2.10). Titles included were 'The Good Things in Life', 'O Sole Mio', 'Passing Strangers', 'End of a Love Affair', 'Oh Lady Be Good', 'Blues for Breakfast', 'Mimi', 'Invitation', 'Someone to Light up My Life', 'It Was You', 'Cute', 'The Midnight Sun', 'London by Night' and a reprise 'The Good Things in Life'.

He had arrived in England on 25 October for the beginning of his three-week Palladium engagement the next day. He brought with him drummer John Cocuzzo, cornetist Ruby Braff and MD John Bunch. On 29 October between shows he dashed to the Finsbury Park Astoria to co-star with Louis Armstrong in a charity variety gala in aid of the National Playing Fields' Association. The two-hour show was hosted by TV personality David Frost and attended by Princess Alexandra.

But while Phonogram had the current Tony Bennett, CBS still had the Bennett song vaults and crossing the new album was their *Tony Bennett's All-Time Greatest Hits*, released in November which contained many of his best known numbers rather than charting titles. Among the tracks were 'The Shadow of Your Smile', 'Put on a Happy Face', 'Boulevard of Broken Dreams', that old favourite of his, 'Stranger in Paradise', and another US million-seller which had preceded his UK popularity, 'Rags to Riches'.

The record was advertised alongside Santana's *Caravan-serai*, Ray Coniff and the Singers' *Love Theme From 'The Godfather'* and *Tequila Sunrise* from David Clayton Thomas.

It was not an unexpected release but sadly it fought with the new material for the time and attention of DJs, programmers and reviewers. Bennett was the unfortunate victim of a prolific past – he had accumulated so much material that a past company would have no problem in re-issuing his product in one form or another. The onus was on Phonogram to ensure that the public realized that they had the new product.

His yearly visits to Britain continued and not surprisingly after the great reaction of 1972 Antonio Dominick Benedetto's early tour in 1973 was heralded as one of the major events for that year even though it had hardly begun. He commenced his tour at the New Theatre, Oxford, on Saturday 24 February and then moved on to the Palladium on Sunday, 25 February before visiting a further eight provincial cities.

People like his record company still spoke of his late 1972 album *The Good Things in Life*, his thirty-first album, and he and Phonogram promoted his latest single 'Living Together, Growing Together'. On his press release for the tour it's interesting to see how attention had still not drifted away from his most memorable recording, 'I Left my Heart in San Francisco'. A number of Tony quotes were marshalled together to show how the song had been written seven years before he had recorded it and how he took six months to get the feel of the song before live audiences prior to his decision that he must commit it to vinyl. For example: 'The record is like a photograph or a thumbprint. I've got to live with it for the rest of my life. When I first heard "Shadow of Your Smile" I spent the whole of a summer trying to get it right then, suddenly, it clicked, and I recorded it.'

123

For this visit Bernie Leighton, whose name and musical talents had been associated with luminaries such as Benny Goodman, Rosemary Clooney, Lena Horne, Frank Sinatra, Bing Crosby, Andy Williams and Pearl Bailey, was announced as the tour's MD and once again the orchestra was to be a thirty-two-piece. And Stateside there was an event of some importance. 'I've heard of backing groups – but this is ridiculous,' Tony Bennett told Pat Doncaster before he left Britain. He was speaking of his club opening at Las Vegas Hilton on 21 May when he would have 107 musicians behind him. 'They are the Nevada Symphony Orchestra. Everybody likes to be first with something in Vegas. And this will be the first time they've had a symphony orchestra in a night club.' The Hilton people got the idea after seeing a telecast of the show Tony did in Britain with the London Philharmonic.

Tony was back in Britain again by the summer and this time the artist who had left his heart in San Francisco toured Britain and with Lena Horne recorded an ATV spectacular to be broadcast on 14 July 1973. *New Reveille* gave him generous coverage but seemed puzzled by him as a person: 'He is not the easiest man to talk to. One minute he is friendly. The next it seems he would prefer just to sit and think. His voice is quiet, and he rarely offers opinions except on the subject of music. Many questions I asked him were followed by a long pause, then: "Right" . . . Was this the man who set a million female hearts fluttering at the sound of his voice? The man who could start a storm of applause merely by singing those opening words: "I left my heart in . . ."? The name who has sold an incredible number of discs and has 250 songs in his personal repertoire? The man whose concerts are always sell-outs almost before they are announced? The man who could ask for, and get, £14,000 a week for a stint in a Northern club?' But later Tony grew chatty and warmed to the proceedings. He was asked whether he might one day retire from performing. 'How can one ever stop? The day I stop learning, when I don't get nervous before a concert, then I shall cease to exist as a singer. I have worked tremendously hard at a relaxed, casual approach in front of the audience. I love being a star. Why shouldn't I say so? I love to entertain people.'

Tony told *New Reveille's*, Margaret Pride, of the advice he was once given by the great Duke Ellington. 'The Duke said to me: "Whatever happens, you must always pick yourself up." That was better than any psychiatrist's advice. Duke considers that man's biggest disease is worrying. He says you should eliminate all negative thinking. It is very difficult, but I keep at it. It is good mental exercise trying not to worry.'

On this occasion he had some forthright comment on the music world of the 1970s. 'Some people make me laugh. They talk about pop stars and how great they are. Mention Bing Crosby or Sinatra and they say "Oh, them." They just don't want to learn. I'm not knocking them, but so many twenty-year-old stars think they know it all and the tragedy is they are boosted up to the skies, only to sink into oblivion and they don't know why.'

A year later he was back in Britain – it was becoming the yearly pilgrimage for Tony – although fans saw it the other way round: a homage paid by a great singer who more than many stars seemed to think it worthwhile to visit Britain regularly and entertain.

His 1974 visit ran from the beginning of March and lasted one week. To coincide with the trip Philips released a single 'All that Love Went to Waste' coupled with 'Some of These Days'. His visit followed extensive club and cabaret work at home. His dates were at London's Festival Hall, 2 March, a concert which was to appear on *Sunday Night at the London Palladium* the following day, the Theatre Club Wakefield on 7 March and two days later at the New Floral Hall, Southport.

The single was written by song-writing genius Sammy Cahn – a multi-million-hit songwriter over the years – with Tony recording the song in America together with the Ruby Braff–George Barnes Quartet and he sang it in his familiar relaxed and warm manner. Tony told Philips: 'If I feel that a concert has not been quite right or that I have been singing below standard then I turn to painting for relief from frustration. In the same way when I become disappointed over painting I seek satisfaction in my singing.' Philips were meanwhile pushing the two LPs they had of Tony's material: *The Good Things in Life* and *Listen Easy*.

In May 1974 he received a special accolade when he was given an Honorary Degree by the Berklee College of Music. President Lawrence Berk, in introducing Tony at the 1974 Baccalaureate Ceremonies on 18 May in the New England Life Hall, said: 'there is hardly a person alive who has not been pleasurably and/or spiritually affected by his unique talent'.

Bennett received an Honorary Doctorate of Music, the first time such an honour had been extended by Berklee to a singer. Tony followed other great names into the college's role of honour – Duke Ellington, Arthur Fiedler and Harry Ellis Dickson. The Commencement Address was given by jazz historian Leonard Feather. Speaking to a full house the noted music critic and syndicated columnist laid much emphasis upon an individual's self-expression. 'It is the artist's duty to . . . remain true to his own beliefs and he must use his acquired knowledge as a point of departure, while remembering that every rule was made to be broken.' He concluded by saying: 'George Dillon . . . once called music "The beautiful disturber of the air". I urge you to go out there and create your disturbance, and may the world discover your beauty.'

The conferring of degrees and diplomas to the Class of 1974 formed the culmination of the ceremonies.

Afterwards *Mrs* Tony Bennett was listed as one of the guests of honour along with Paul T. Tierney of the Boston School Committee; Musicians' Association President Sam Marcus, and Peter C. Sireagusa, Music Adviser of Boston Public Schools.

It was a memorable and rewarding day and many present felt that Leonard Feather's remarks found a true expression in the philosophy and career of Tony Bennett.

By November 1974 Tony was once more pulling in the Stateside as he and Lena Horne again toured and shared the stage. *Variety* magazine of 6 November noted: 'None of the bookers in the Loew's State Era when six acts on a bill was normal would have believed that one day it would be possible to get a $15 top for only two performers. Today it's not only possible, but in the case of Tony (Bennett) and Lena (Horne) which opened for a two-and-a-half week run at the Minskoff, it's prime musical entertainment that deserves high marks at the box-office.'

Lena sang the first half with her customary and expected skill and had Robert Freedman conducting. *Variety* described her as a lady who 'slinks, slithers and sings. She cannot miss.' Tony sang the second half and for the famed US show-biz journal it was clearly evident that here was a professional who was aware of his strengths and navigated accordingly. 'Bennett's tunes are generally familiar and melodic. He seems equally at home outside of San Francisco, where he left his heart some years ago, as he is with tunes from Broadway and Tin Pan Alley. He is an excellent craftsman.'

The closing manoeuvre saw both Tony and Lena singing tunes by Harold Arlen, who was introduced from the audience. *Variety's* man thought it was a device that closed the show on an extremely high note. Tony was accompanied by a philharmonic-size orchestra with Robert Freedman's opposite in the Bennett camp being the familiar Torrie Zito.

In March 1975 he was sharing the spotlight once more with Lena Horne at the Schubert Theater, Los Angeles. It was again a perfect marriage for ticket hunters and music lovers wanting an entire evening of magic. When Lena commenced her set after a short duet with Tony, she soon commanded attention from her basic movement to the way in which she blended musicianship and personality and took charge of the proceedings.

The *Los Angeles Times* for Friday, 21 March 1975, saw the Bennett set establishing the show as a dual triumph rather than as a duel of egos. They thought he was less inclined to mix contemporary songs with the great standards if his choice might be compared with Ms Horne. The only really new item was 'Life Is Beautiful', with music by Fred Astaire and words by Tommy Wolfe. The orchestra was used extensively and intelligently with solo space left to be well taken by the likes of saxophonist Harold Land and Pete Christlieb. In Lena's act guitarist Gabor Szabo was given a prominent place and both brought out the best in trumpeter Blue Mitchell. The newspaper's famed writer Leonard Feather commented: 'Bennett singing "For Once in My Life" or gliding from a flawlessly sustained top note to a tender gently closing phrase on the enchanting "Lost in the Stars" is the epitome of style, top quality popular music, of impeccable taste and refusal to compromise. He can even bring significance, or at least an irresistible beat, to such a chestnut as "There'll Be Some Changes Made" from your prehistoric Hit Parade of 1921.'

The finale saw Bennett joined by Lena Horne for the singing of some twenty excerpts from Harold Arlen songs. It was class; it was buoyant musical presentation.

In June 1975 the new UK LP was *Let's Fall In Love with the Songs of Harold Arlen and Cy Coleman*. British CBS declared: 'And you really can't afford to turn down an invitation like that from Tony Bennett for when one of the greatest vocal talents in the world sings the songs of two of the best composers, you come up with an album that is DYNAMITE!'

The album was a double set of Tony firstly singing songs of Cy Coleman, famed for compositions like 'The Best Is Yet to Come', 'It Amazes Me', 'Then Was Then and Now Is Now' and 'I've Got the Number' from the Broadway musical *Little Me*, and then songs by Harold Arlen, who in his time had written such classics as 'The Man that Got Away', 'Somewhere over the Rainbow', 'I've Got the World on a String' and 'Come Rain or Come Shine'.

In May 1976 he was back in Britain sharing the billing with Lena. There was a brief coming together of kindred natures as they came on stage and launched into George Harrison's 'Something'. There followed the tender, haunting number 'The Look of Love', known to many British listeners for a version by Dusty Springfield, and 'My Funny Valentine'. Lena Horne proceeded to take the stage and run through a programme of nineteen songs with Tony following before there was another coming-together. *Sunday Times* writer, Derek Jewell, told his millions of readers: 'Bennett was even more surprising. He was once a rather rasping singer I could take or leave. Last year he broke with the CBS empire after making an incredible seventy-eight albums, set up his own record company and is in renaissance. He's been singing with Woody Herman's band and it shows. Suddenly he's a swinger. He rode the waves of the sparkling orchestra like a champion surfer, counterpointing with the brass, encouraging the players to solo. His voice is richer-toned and, I'd swear, boasting an extra octave. Maybe this is an illusion. No matter. Bennett was brilliant, reminding us he'd left his heart in San Francisco but, more importantly, signalling where his heart now resides by concentrating all his artistry into a breathtaking trio of Ellington songs.

'It was over too soon. Lena Horne perhaps shouldn't

waste her time on Paul Williams. Bennett put not a foot wrong. There was no competition between magnificent artists, only empathy. They should do it more often.'

Later in the month Tony was in Vegas with Basie and causing the usual flurry of excited reviews. US critic Forrest Duke exclaimed that 'the blend of all-time-great supertalents is so smooth, so intoxicating, and tasty it should be bottled for posterity'. Bennett had the crowds hopping up repeatedly to give him standing ovations and Forrest said: 'Charming and sex-appealing, singing a programme that couldn't be bettered, Tony's zesty delivery makes every number a delicacy.' Tony's repertoire included 'I Wish I Were in Love Again', 'The Good Things in Life', a blockbuster rendering of 'I Want to Be Around to Pick up the Pieces', 'There'll Be Some Changes Made', a medley of his hits and the Bennett–Basie segment together where they paid tribute to Ellington. Basie played the piano.

In November he was booked into the Natural History Museum's Baird Auditorium (the second event in the Smithsonian's American Popular Song series) and caused the writer of the *Washington Post* to exclaim: 'There are times when a popular performance crosses that thin line which separates serious personal art from superior entertainment.' With Bennett providing the latter the *Post* writer described him as the 'best male/jazz popular singer we have'. And the uncredited reviewer added: 'The new twist is that he appears to be less than content with that title. Tony Bennett is attempting, it seems, to be better than excellent, and it looks as if he's succeeding.'

It will come as no surprise to learn that his programme took in his repertoire from the past twenty-five years. He closed the proceedings by asking the packed audience in the auditorium whether they would like a memory of Al Jolson as he and pianist Torrie Zito rendered 'Sunny Side of the Street'. The *Washington Post* expressed the feelings of so many when it closed its report by saying: 'It would have been impossible to think of a better ending.'

By 1977 Tony's career was displaying definite changes of direction or, at least, a greater diversity. He had been developing his artistic interests over many years but now, in London, on 7 November 1977, he opened an exhibition of his paintings at the Milne-Henderson Gallery at 99 Mount Street, London, W1. The gallery was opened to the public and proceeds from the exhibition, which ran for two weeks, were donated to the Variety Club of Great Britain.

Bennett was busy in other ways – he had flown in at the beginning of the month to record his own television 'special' for Granada, the Manchester centred independent television company, which also had offices in London. He was accompanied by one of Britain's most popular big bands, the Syd Lawrence Orchestra, and so for the first time Tony and a British band worked together. Lawrence's band had in the 1970s become one of the nation's most popular outfits with the recreation of style and sound associated with Glen Miller. Lawrence – a former member of the BBC's famed Northern Dance Orchestra – had formed his band in 1968. Their first major break had come in November 1969 when the orchestra played before a capacity audience at London's Royal Festival Hall. Numerous radio and television bookings had followed.

In addition to the television special, Tony also played a shortish British tour with the Syd Lawrence Orchestra. Presented by Tito Burns he booked in at London's Theatre Royal, Drury Lane, for the opening concert and then moved on to Croydon, Leicester, Stockport, Southport, Derby, Harrogate, Gloucester, Eastbourne and Cambridge.

In 1978 there was much to celebrate for he found himself accorded a special honour by the Fashion

Foundation of America. On Monday, 16 January 1978, they issued their list of 'America's Best Dressed Men' in eleven fields in their 39th annual survey of custom tailors and designers. The selections were based on individual style, taste, budget and occupation and the awards were intended to encourage better design for better living. President Jimmy Carter won the 'Statesman' category, President Anwar Sadat of Egypt, the 'International Government' and under 'Entertainment', the man himself. For winning his category Tony received a medal symbolic of his 'Best-Dressed' selection and was enrolled in the Fashion Foundation of America's Hall of Fashion Fame. Previous awards had gone to stars like Bob Hope and Frank Sinatra.

In that same year the US journal *People* told readers that the fifty-two-year old singer was getting up to $10,000 for his acrylics and since most of the purchasers were fans he had taken to exhibiting his work in concert-hall lobbies. During a one-week engagement in Chicago's Drury Lane he had sold two paintings with a third of the proceeds earmarked for charity. *People Weekly* thought his selling was helped by the Old Master-sounding signature on the canvas: Tony's given name – Antonio Benedetto.

'Painting has a relationship with music, you know. Like all arts, painting has line, form and colour. You go through a rollercoaster effect when you're painting. All those emotions . . . scratch, scratch, it's almost a form of meditation.' To Tony the best painters around in Hollywood were Henry Fonda and Elke Sommer.

But of course the singing was also flourishing, with critical acclaim becoming ever more unstinted, outdoing even the superlatives of past years. During 1978 there was one stunning review after another with particularly fulsome admiration coming from the *Toronto Star*, on 24 October, the morning after his concert at the Royal Alexandra Theatre. He was termed, quite simply: 'The

Mercedes of classical pop singers', and then seen as invariably: 'dependable, classy to a fault and exquisitely fine-tuned. But unlike almost all cars, no matter how expensive, Bennett continues to improve and possess more life and character as he grows older.'

Only the second solo singer to perform for some time at the venue, Tony gave a different set of songs for each of the six nights he was booked. The first half of each show had a different theme while the second half was devoted to his standards. He was backed for the first half by the Chicago String Ensemble and among his six different song menus was his version of the great movie music of past years. It ranged from 'I Wish I Were in Love Again' to Charlie Chaplin's 'Smile'.

Writer Bruce Blackadar was stunned by Bennett's vocal dexterity: 'With a raspy voice that so often seems to be on the verge of breaking before it amazes you two notes later with its power'. He was concerned to stress that one of the joys of a Bennett show was a total lack of 'downers' for every song had class treatment and was 'revived, renewed and refreshed' by the singer's unique talent: 'What's so astounding about Bennett is his consistent sincerity. There's not a false note in his show, no snappy one-liners to loosen up the audience. He's a master of economy; he has stripped away every frill and presents only the gold.' Blackadar noticed: 'the audience, most of whom appeared to be middle-aged, purred with instant recognition almost from the first bar of each song.'

There was – not surprisingly – a similar report on the second half where the numbers would have been slightly more familiar, although of course much, if not all, of the first half represented numbers culled from various Bennett recordings and then assembled under a thematic guise. In the show's second half Bennett was accompanied by a rousing thirty-two-piece orchestra. The blockbuster finale was an evocative medley of 'Autumn

Leaves' and 'When the World Was Young'. It was – as Blackadar wrote – class, and class always shows.

By 1979 US writers and observers were noticing how Bennett was circumventing the established system. The 'normal' practice lay in an artist making major television programmes for one of the three big US TV companies – ABC, NBC, CBS – or at least that was the theory, for in most cases it meant that an artist had to wait for the big break or a rebooking. But it was observed that Bennett was achieving as much TV coverage through other means as even some of the popular US series such as *Charlie's Angels* or *The Jeffersons*. Bennett was busy making programmes for foreign television, PBS and Cable TV. It was a case of finding visual routes other than the accepted channels where the door may be closed. Often his success in obtaining coverage was due to the fact that he was not offering the so-called popularity which comes from hit records, where the 'chart' placing is considered more important than quality, and instant fan appeal is seen as denoting real ability.

'The networks will soon have to come down off their high horse. As cable TV becomes more popular the networks won't be all that powerful any more. People are just realizing that the air is free. We never knew that before. The networks always made us believe we had to go through them.

'There are some pretty adventurous guys in the TV business who are hitting the satellite from local stations and creating instant networks. There could be about fifty networks within a year and a half and there will be plenty of selectivity. There will be some terrible things, but there will also be a lot of wonderful educational things.'

Bennett was aware that his fellow entertainers felt that the networks had little disposition to devote prime-time programming to variety shows but he advised them not to fall victim to their cynicism. He found common empathy

134

with critics who felt the companies manipulated the public rather than vice-versa and that in so doing, even with good faith, they misunderstood the needs and wants of the people.

'I believe in what Richard Rodgers told me: "The audience is the critic." The truth is the public loves to see great performers. When I did the Carson show the other night there was a flute player named Jim Galway who absolutely stopped the show cold with his marvellous playing. This kind of music is exactly the opposite of what Madison Avenue says the public will like.'

And in common with many US performers then and now he felt that some foreign television systems had greater interest in presenting class musical shows. 'Britain has always opened its doors to me. I've done specials for the company. Any time I've had a good idea, they said, "Let's do it." I received an offer from Global Television in Rio de Janeiro. If I decide to go down there they'll turn the whole network over to me, with all their facilities – anything I want to do. In Switzerland they just said, "Consider this is your home. You're welcome here anytime you want to do a television show."'

In 1979 Tony recorded six prime-time shows for BBC-TV and when he arrived in the country for his recordings he was quick to exclaim on seeing oceans of mail awaiting: 'It's amazing how my family keeps on growing. The bond I have with them is something special. They confide in me and treat me like an old friend. I love it. Years ago Sophie Tucker told me to go to London because she said the audiences were something special. I had played in New York, the West Coast and Las Vegas and I thought I could really read audiences. But I soon found that London and Britain is different. I think it is the responsiveness that comes through. You feel people are really keen to see and hear you and they have a desire to listen to good music. Now I tend to look on Britain as a second home and I enjoy working with the BBC. I am always on the move. I suppose that has been my whole life. I am rarely at home in Los Angeles. I sometimes get confused because when I wake up I forget where I am. But it is a lovely life and I am a very lucky man. Sure, I love Britain. They're spectacular people. They always pull through.

'I have many stories of the British but I have a favourite one of a twelve-year-old girl whose father took her to the Palladium. She asked me to do a Rodgers and Hart album. Last time I was there, I drove up in one of those chauffeured limousines, and there she was, holding up the album against the window. She's become engaged and married and did so on the condition her husband lets her play her Tony Bennett albums! Now that's satisfaction. You know, 98 per cent of the time, I can't wait to hit the stage. Then I just love to see the audience struttin' out afterwards.'

He reckoned he had sung almost a thousand songs on his nearly a hundred released albums and said songs came to him at a rate of a thousand every month. 'Everyone you meet thinks they can write a hit song. They arrive by the sackful and I try to listen to most of them. I rarely find one I want but that doesn't mean I stop looking.'

For his six BBC shows Bennett adopted a pattern similar to the one already described for some of his American nightclub acts. Each of the six shows was devoted to a different theme. The first of the series centred on Tin Pan Alley and others focussed on Broadway hits and film songs. He promised some new material but admitted his personal preferences: 'I'm really a Twenties and Thirties man.' He did, however, include songs from several British writers, McCartney and Harrison amongst them. In the first show he included standards like 'Pennies from Heaven', 'If I Ruled the World', 'It Had to Be You', and

136

numbers by Fats Waller. In his 'film' programme he sang among others, 'This Time' from *Cabaret*, Charlie Chaplin's 'Smile' and two songs written for Fred Astaire – 'They Can't Take That Away from Me' and 'One for the Road'.

Aside from his singing prowess and aspirations there was minor controversy over two things. He was critical of Barry Manilow – fast becoming the precious star and friend to thousands of mainly British women – by saying singers like him 'come out of the ice-box' and doubting whether they had the background or dedication to stay the course as long as he (Bennett) has. He referred to his upbringing and told again of how his first professional bookings came as a waiter at a tough waterfront café: 'When the customers asked for a song you had to know it or else'. 'The only secret is hard work. I work as hard today as when I started out back in New York. Guys like Sinatra and Bob Hope are around today because they know the value of working. They believe in perfection and it shows. The pros always come back.'

And there was the question of what had happened to him up yonder – meaning his head! Bennett had said at his press conference: 'I haven't changed over the years.' But he changed his hairstyle, it was noticed! When he appeared on TV he sported some semblance of an Afro hairdo and the question asked by the more show-biz-gossip-orientated section of the British press was quite simple: 'Where has this sudden mop of black curly hair come from? Is it a toupée? Is it a transplant?' The calls of the press to Tony's office met with little enthusiasm and a distinct lack of cooperation: 'It is Mr Bennett's own business,' was the curt reply, and some parts of the British press were miffed.

The TV series had a great reception, with countless appreciative letters flooding in to the BBC – it was a fitting way for him to end another decade, his third as a star name and fourth in the business.

Tony Bennett had again outlasted the vagaries and whims of popular music's ever shifting musical foundations and indeed his very assault on the TV restrictions imposed by the major companies had more than anything proved something already displayed by the 'full house' signs at concerts and clubs – that here was an artist whom the public adored and wanted to see and hear but who had all too often been neglected in favour of 'hit' performers who could only sing against the backcloth of a tape.

Tony Bennett was ready for the 1980s!

7.

The 1980s

FOURTH DECADE Tony Bennett may be a little older, wiser, and his face is much thinner, with extra lines creasing its contours, but he remains in the front rank of American pop artists and some would say he is the heir apparent to Sinatra. Much time has elapsed since one critic remarked in April 1950 that he was 'another cherubic Italian mama's boy with a bad case of frogs'. In contrast, New York disc jockey Bob Jones remarked in the autumn of 1980: 'I think he's inevitable (as a successor) today as Sinatra was when Bing Crosby was everybody's favourite singer.' In the 1980s Bennett has consolidated his hold on the affections of lovers of good music and more so he has written himself into the 'all-time-great' league by being the star guest at several functions which have achieved world-wide reportage. He sang at a lavish reception thrown by President Reagan for the British monarchy and he journeyed to Britain for his part in a special televised and star-studded tribute to Duke Ellington at St Paul's Cathedral, London, where the great man's sacred music was played, sung and even danced to.

Stateside there were several major events to open the decade. He starred in a special US network television film *A Gift of Love* in which he played the part of a clown. Mario Pellegrini, producer-director, when asked why he chose Bennett, said: 'We didn't want a slick Hollywood type. We needed sincerity. And that's what Tony Bennett is about.' The film's profits went to United Way. Another momentous event was Bennett's decision to take the plunge, form his own record company and run his own affairs.

'I'm setting it up with my sons,' he said. The two sons came from his first marriage and were Danny, now twenty-six, and Daegal, twenty-two, both based in New Jersey and also members of their own group, Neon. The long-time artist said he had had enough of the ramifications of doing it the so-called proper way and now 'it's going to be a corner grocery operation, not a chainstore supermarket'. Bennett said he had been under pressure for years to produce the 'hits'. 'There was a time when I had to turn one out every six weeks, like clockwork. The biggies corrupt your albums. Every song has to be a hit. But they aren't personal victories. You lose your continuity and your timing, working like that. And you lose your identity. The trouble is, the big companies don't know how to deal with honesty, like Charlie Chaplin said.'

Tony – who appeared at the decade's opening at the Fairmont Hotel, San Francisco – said during his residency that he was not into the false trappings of show-biz and indeed on that occasion he was in a casual grey suit and an open shirt, the only sign of show-biz and affluence being a silk scarf knotted around his neck. 'I don't market myself,' he declared and said 'they' have done so. 'Just look though at the marketing geniuses of the business. One month, they're on top. Next month they're a disaster area. It's what Norman Mailer called "The American insanity".'

But undoubtedly Tony's disaffection with the record company moguls has affected both his sales and his career. The problem for the 'small' concern lies not only in finding original marketing techniques to establish the record, or in organizing distribution but in having insufficient manpower to make the many markets, especially the media, aware of a release. And his records have not fared as successfully as they have done through the two majors with which he's been associated, but arguably the principle is more important, and intertwined with this is the need for artistic satisfaction and creative honesty.

The American was in Britain at the outset of the 1980s, and particularly well received was his short tour in 1982 which took him to several major centres in the country including two concerts at the Royal Festival Hall in London. The tour was presented by Peter Brightman, Brian Theobald and IMCP. He came with a small orchestra under his musical director Ralph Sharon. He brought with him John Burr on bass and Joe LaBarbara on drums, augmented by British musicians Jim McLeod and John Allan on violins, Don McKay viola and Nigel Warren-Green on 'cello. Ticket prices were most reasonable. For the Manchester concert at the Free Trade Hall on 1 March they were priced at £6.50. £5.50, £4.50 and £3 – a far cry from the prices charged by other US quality artists.

The critical reaction was still favourable, often the reviews full of warm, glowing praise. He was seen as the last of the crooners, a bar-room singer in a tight tuxedo with a mean line in melody. *Daily Mail's* Patrick O'Neill commented: 'I have seen Sinatra and Bennett on stage in the past six months. Tony has less charisma, but more hair – and he's in better voice.

'If Sinatra is Ol' Blue Eyes, Bennett is Mister Punch. A man with all the bellicose seductive qualities of the puppet whose profile he shares. He takes them to the moon, reminds them that a kiss is still a kiss and life is still 'swonderful, 'smarvellous.'

Gerald Dempsey in the *Daily Express* called him the old seducer, wooing his victims with soft talk but shaping the musical phrases like a sculptor. For Ray King in Britain's major selling provincial, the *Manchester Evening News*, Bennett's performance could be summed up by the word 'subtlety' and King saw the evening as ideal for fans whose concentration was geared towards vocal style and interpretation. He heard a sweet, husky voice that was occasionally lost in the lower registers but had perfect phrasing and timing. King found that there was only minimal amplification and compared the set-up with a Vegas-style presentation as offering a complete contrast, for with a lack of obvious amplifications in Bennett's performance there was also an absence of lights except for spots and footlights. But whatever was or was not missing there remained the incomparable quality of Bennett the artist.

So here in the 1980s Bennett remained a superb vocal craftsman with his whole show saluting the love of good music, and he was to emphasize his sense of the importance of the music in relation to himself by introducing musical director Sharon during the first number! His approach to his audience showed no change: it was clean and simple, and even without the backup singers, the big orchestra or the band he was able to take the words of songs and make them stand out along the skyline of his music as clearly and boldly as the skyscrapers in San Francisco. The words continue to be the warm words, the embracing words, the ironic words of love.

It was said in previous decades and it has been repeated in the 1980s that what you get when Tony Bennett sings are classic love songs done in classic style and anyone who attends a concert without that in mind can only receive a jolt. Bennett in the past, outside his early pop chart days, has never made any concessions to keep pace with a 'current fad' and the 1980s have seen a continuance of this policy.

It still stands true in the early 1980s that he ensures love is with the audience from the commencement of his show. 'He also introduces us to his unique style; he's not just a singer, he's an actor who happens to work in music instead of theatre. No matter what the tempo, the message is always a picture of delightful, swirling, floating love. His vocal range is astonishing and he's equally at home whether singing love songs, swinging with a big band or working with a quartet. He sings, then speaks in a soft voice, then whispers some syllables. At the end of the show he even sits alone without a microphone on a stool with no one but his music director stroking a piano in the background. There is a tremendous subtle quality in performing this way, making each note a vital link in a delicate chain. This is what he chooses as a highlight and an encore.' But there's much more to it than that, which is scarcely surprising, for anyone who is at the top of the tree can only stay there because people realize that even the highest acclaim cannot fully describe an artist who himself keeps maturing like good wine.

These days Tony has become increasingly concerned to lend his talents for the benefit of numerous causes, so much so that he has become known as 'Tony Benefit' among his peers. He has averaged fifty charity concerts a year. He has maintained his popularity because even the least of persons has been regarded as highly as the best paid, most famous and most influential music promoters. Bennett is known as the singer who finds time for disc jockeys in the smallest towns and cities he visits – people often neglected by the superstars.

'Why shouldn't I drop in on a small station if the guy is playing the kind of music we're both interested in?' he exclaimed on one such occasion.

The 1980s are his – and he's in his fourth decade of greatness.

PART THREE

Record and Song Reference

THIS RECORD AND song reference section follows a simple pattern.

Singles and EPs run in number sequence and albums follow suit. The album section consists of main LP release listings and these are followed by details of the many budget-priced and special sets of his material.

After the various discographies there is an A to Z of song titles recorded on singles, EPs and, separately, LPs. This A to Z should aid those who wonder whether Tony Bennett sang such and such a song and on which record it can be located.

Much of the material listed here is no longer in available catalogues but numerous stores carry deleted material and, for the enquirer seeking albums and singles that can no longer be ordered, there is no alternative but to hunt around.

8.

Singles and EPs

Columbia (COL.)

DB 2789 'Our Lady of Fatima' (w. Chorus cond. Norman Leyden); 'Just Say I Love Her' (w. Orch. cond. Marty Manning).

DB 2924 'Cold, Cold Heart'; 'Because of You' (w. Orch. cond. Percy Faith).

DB 2972 'I Won't Cry Anymore'; 'Blue Velvet' (w. Orch. cond. Percy Faith).

DB 2988 'While We're Young' (w. Percy Faith and his Orchestra) 'I Can't Give You Anything But Love' (w. Orch. dir. Marty Manning).

DB 3101 'Somewhere Along the Way'; 'Since My Love Has Gone (w. Percy Faith and his Orchestra).

DB 3178 'You Could Make Me Smile Again'; 'Have a Good Time' (w. Percy Faith and his Orchestra).

DB 3198 'Stay Where You Are' (w. Percy Faith and his Orchestra); 'Anywhere I Wander' (w. Percy Faith and his Orchestra and Chorus).

DB 3295 or SCM 5048 'Take Me' (w. Percy Faith and his Orchestra); 'Congratulations to Someone' (w. Percy Faith and his Orchestra and Chorus).

Philips

PB 216 'Rags to Riches'; 'No One Will Ever Know' (w. Percy Faith and his Orchestra).

PB 267 'Here Comes that Heartache Again'; 'There'll Be No Teardrops Tonight' (w. Percy Faith and his Orchestra).

PB 322 'Until Yesterday'; 'Cinnamon Sinner' (w. Percy Faith and his Orchestra).

PB 357　'Madonna, Madonna'; 'Not as a Stranger' (w. Percy Faith and his Orchestra).

PB 390　'Please Driver'; 'Funny Thing' (w. Percy Faith and his Orchestra).

PB 420　'Stranger in Paradise' (w. Percy Faith and his Orchestra and Chorus); 'Take me back again' (w. Percy Faith and his Orchestra).

PB 445　'Close Your Eyes' (w. Chorus and Orchestra); 'It's Too Soon to Know' (w. Orchestra).

PB 477　'Punch and Judy Love'; 'Kisses I'll Never Forget' (w. Percy Faith and his Orchestra).

PB 486　'Don't Tell Me Why'; 'May I Never Love Again' (w. Percy Faith and his Orchestra).

PB 521　'How Can I Replace You'; 'Tell Me that You Love Me' (w. Percy Faith and his Orchestra).

PB 537　'Come Next Spring'; 'Afraid of the Dark' (w. Percy Faith and his Orchestra).

PB 563　'Capri in May'; 'Sing You Sinners' (w. Percy Faith and his Orchestra).

PB 501　'Can You Find It in Your Heart'; 'Forget Her' (w. Percy Faith and his Orchestra).

PB 628　'Happiness Street' (w. Percy Faith and his Orchestra); 'From the Candy Store on the Corner to the Chapel on the Hill' (w. Lois Winter (voc) and Percy Faith and his Orchestra and Chorus).

PB 672　'Heart'; 'Whatever Lola Wants (Lola gets)' (w. Orch. cond. Sid Feller).

PB 689　'Sold to the Man with the Broken Heart'; 'One Kiss Away from Heaven' (w. Percy Faith and his Orchestra).

PB 710　'No Hard Feelings' (w. Percy Faith and his Orchestra); 'One for my Baby' (w. Ray Conniff and his Orchestra).

PB 724　'In the middle of an Island'; 'I am' (w. Ray Ellis and his Orchestra).

PB 753　'Ça, c'est l'amour' (w. Neal Hefti and his Orchestra); 'Just in Time' (w. Percy Faith and his Orchestra).

PB 786　'I Never Felt More Like Falling in Love' (w. Ray Ellis and his Orchestra); 'Love Me, Love Me, Love Me' (w. Percy Faith and his Orchestra).

PB 831 or 45　'Young and Warm and Wonderful'; 'Now I Lay

148

Me Down to Sleep' (w. Frank De Vol and his Orchestra).

PB 855 or 45 'Firefly'; 'Night that Heaven Fell' (w. Ray Ellis and his Orchestra and Chorus).

PB 907 or 45 'It's so Peaceful in the Country' (w. Ralph Sharon and his Orchestra); 'Being True to One Another' (w. Glenn Osser and his Orchestra).

PB 961 or 45 'You Can't Love 'em All'; 'Smile' (w. Ralph Burns and his Orchestra).

45PB 996 'Love Look Away' (w. Glenn Osser and his Orchestra); 'Cool School' (w. Ralph Sharon and his Orchestra).

45PB 1008 'I'll Bring You a Rainbow'; 'Ask Me (I Know)' (w. Orchestra Cond. Frank de Vol).

45PB 1079 'Ask Anyone in Love' (w. Ralph Burns and his Orchestra); 'Till' (w. Orch. cond. Frank De Vol).

45PB 1089 'Marriage-go-round'; 'Somebody' (w. accom. cond. Glenn Osser).

45PB 1122 'Climb Ev'ry Mountain' (w. Orch. and Chorus cond. Frank De Vol); 'Ramona' (w. Orch. cond. by Glenn Osser).

PB 1149 'Baby, Talk to Me'; 'Put on a Happy Face' (w. Orch. cond. Frank de Vol).

PB 1218 'The Best Is Yet to Come'; 'Tender Is the Night' (w. Orch. cond. by Marty Manning).

BBE 12009 'Stranger in Paradise'; 'Take Me Back Again' (w. Percy Faith and his Orchestra & Chorus). 'May I Never Love Again'; 'Punch and Judy Love' (w. Percy Faith and his Orchestra).

BBE 12145 'In the middle of an Island' (part side) (w. Ray Ellis and his Orchestra).

BBE 12148 'Just in Time' (part side) (w. Percy Faith and his Orchestra).

BBE 12159 'Just in Time' (w. Percy Faith and his Orchestra); 'One for my Baby' (w. Ray Conniff and his Orchestra); 'Ça, C'est l'Amour' (w. Neal Hefti and his Orchestra); 'In the Middle of an Island' (w. Ray Ellis and his Orchestra).

BBE 12223 'Firefly' (w. Ray Ellis and his Orchestra); 'I Fall in Love too Easily' (w. Chuck Wayne (guitar) and instrumental accomp.); 'It Had to Be You'; 'Boulevard of Broken Dreams' (w. Orch. dir. by Ray Conniff).

BBE 12338 'The Skyscraper Blues'; 'Penthouse Serenade (When We're Alone)' (w. Orch. dir. Ralph Burns).

BBE 12424 'Marriage-Go-Round'; 'Somebody' (w. Orch. cond. by Glenn Osser); 'Ask anyone in love' (w. Ralph Burns and his Orchestra); 'Till' (w. Accompaniment dir. Frank De Vol).

BBE 12437 'Climb Ev'ry Mountain' (part side) (w. Orch. and Chorus cond. Frank de Vol).

BBE 12461 'Alone Together'; 'This Is All I Ask'; 'After You've Gone'; 'How Long Has This Been Going On'.

6006 309 'The Good Things in Life' (w. Orch. cond. Robert Farnon); 'Love Is the Thing' (w. Orch. cond. Don Costa).

6006 326 'Give Me Love (Give Me Peace On Earth)'; 'My Love' (w. Orch. cond. Torrie Zito).

6006 372s 'All That Love Went to Waste' (from the film *A Touch of Class*); 'Some of these days' (w. Orch. cond. Torrie Zito).

CBS

AAG 121 or 201730 'I Left my Heart in San Francisco'; 'Candy Kisses' (w. Orch. dir. Marty Manning).

AAG 126 'Marry Young' (w. Orch. cond. Cy Coleman); 'You'll Never Get Away from Me' (w. Ralph Sharon and his Orch.).

AAG 137 or 201733 'I Wanna Be Around'; 'I Will Live my Life for You' (w. Orch. cond. Marty Manning).

AAG 153 'The Good Life' (w. Orch. dir. Marty Manning); 'Spring in Manhattan' (w. Orch. and Chorus cond. Don Costa).

AAG 165 'True Blue Lou' (w. Chorus and Orch.); 'This is All I Ask' (w. Chorus and Orch. cond. Ralph Burns.)

AAG 176 'Don't Wait Too Long'; 'Limehouse Blues' (w. Orch. cond. Dick Hyman).

AAG 184 'The Little Boy' (w. Orch. cond. Dick Hyman); 'The moment of Truth' (w. Orch. cond. Ralph Burns).

AAG 191 'The Kid's a Dreamer' (w. Orch. cond. Dick Hyman and Bobby Hackett (cornet); 'When Joanna Loved Me' (w. Orch. cond. Marty Manning).

AAG 208 'Follow Me' (w. Orch. cond. Glenn Osser); 'Soon It's gonna Rain' (w. Ralph Sharon Trio).

AAG 225 'Who Can I Turn To?' (w. Orch.); 'Corcovado (Quiet Night)' (w. Orch. cond. Marty Manning).

2779 'Keep Smiling at Trouble'; 'Days of Love' (w. Orch.

cond. Marion Evans).

2970 'Country Girl' (w. Orch. cond. Marion Evans); 'Baby Dream Your Dream' (w. Orch. cond. David Rose).

3064 'For Once in My Life'; 'How Do You Say Auf Wiedersehn' (w. Orch. cond. Torrie Zito).

3370 'The Glory of Love' (w. his San Francisco Buddy Dominic Germano) (vocal group); 'A Fool of Fools' (both with Orch. cond. Torrie Zito).

3573 'Yesterday I Heard the Rain (Esta tarde vi llover)'; 'Sweet Georgie Fame' (w. Orch. conducted by Torrie Zito).

3731 'Hushabye Mountain' (with Ernie Calabria, guitar); 'Hi-Ho' (both with Orch. cond. by Torrie Zito).

4092 'They All Laughed', 'People' (w. instru. accomp. cond. Torrie Zito).

4224 'Play It Again Sam' (w. Marky Markowitz, trumpet); 'What the World Needs Now is Love' (both w. Orch. cond. Torrie Zito).

4527 'I've Gotta Be Me'; 'A Lonely Place' (from film *Heaven with a Gun*) (w. Orch. cond. Torrie Zito).

S 4958s 'Little Green Apples'; 'Something' (w. Orch.).

S 5255s 'MacArthur Park'; 'Eleanor Rigby' (w. Orch.).

S 5307s 'I'll Begin Again' (w. Orch. cond. Torrie Zito); 'My Cherie Amour' (w. Orch.).

S 7056s 'Where Do I Begin' (theme from *Love Story*); 'Tea for Two' (w. Orch.)

S 7342s 'More and More'; 'I want to Be Happy' (w. Orch.).

S 7535s 'Walkabout – Theme from the film'; 'How Beautiful Is Night' (w. Orch. cond. Robert Farnon).

S 7711s 'The Summer Knows'; 'Somewhere Along the Line' (w. Orch. cond. Torrie Zito).

7984 'Twilight World/Easy Come, Easy Go'.

S 8095s 'More and more'; 'Maybe this time' (w. Orch.).

1143 CBS Hall of Fame 'I Left My Heart in San Francisco'/'The Good Life'.

EP 6066 *When Joanna Loved Me*: 'When Joanna loved me' (w. Orch. cond. Marty Manning); 'This is All I ask' (w. Chorus and Ralph Burns and his Orchestra); 'In other words (Fly Me to the Moon)' (w. the Will Bronson Singers and Orch. cond. Don Costa); 'A Taste of Honey' (w. Orch. cond. Dick Hyman).

EP 6071   *Till*: 'Till'; 'September Song'; 'Speak Low'; 'We musn't Say Goodbye (w. Orch. cond. Frank De Vol).

EP 6151   *The Best of Bennett*: 'I left my Heart in San Franciso' (w. Orch. cond. Marty Manning); 'The Very Thought of You' (w. Bobby Hackett (trumpet) and Orch. cond. Johnny Keating); 'If I ruled the World' (w. Will Bronson Singers and Orch. cond. Don Costa); 'Who Can I Turn To?' (w. Orch.).

201735   'If I ruled the World' (w. Will Bronson Chorus and Orch. cond. Don Costa); 'Who can I turn to?' (w. Orch. cond. George Siravo).

202021   'Sleepy Time Gal'; 'The Very Thought of You' (w. Bobby Hackett (trumpet) and Orch. cond. Johnny Keating).

202084   'Second Time Around'; 'Shadow of Your Smile' (w. Orch. cond. Johnny Mandel).

202346   'A Time for Love' (w. Orch. cond. Johnny Mandel); 'Georgia Rose' (w. Orch. cond. Ralph Burns).

AGG 20037   *The Good Life*: 'The Good Life'; 'Quiet Nights' (w. Orch. cond. Marty Manning); 'Until I Met You' (w. The Ralph Sharon Trio); 'Blue Velvet' (w. Ralph Sharon and his Orch.).

AGG 20052   *The Moment of Truth*: 'The Moment of Truth' (w. Orch. cond. Ralph Burns); 'So Long, Big Time' (w. Orch. cond. Harold Arlen); 'Young and Foolish' (w. Chorus and Orch. cond. Ralph Burns); 'Caravan' (w. Chico Hamilton (drums) and Orch. cond. Ralph Sharon).

9

LPs

Philips

BBL 7138   *Tony Bennett Showcase*: It had to be You; You Can Depend on Me; I'm Just a Lucky So and So; Taking a Chance on Love; These Foolish Things; I Can't Give You Anything but Love/Boulevard of Broken Dreams; I'll Be Seeing You; Always; Love Walked In; Lost in the Stars; Without a Song (w. Orch. dir. Ray Conniff; Percy Faith and his Orch. and Chorus).

Philips; BBL 7219; Harmony: HS 11340s*   *The Beat of My Heart/ Just One of Those Things**: Let's Begin[+]; Just One of Those Things (featuring Art Blakey (drums)); Lullaby of Broadway; Army Air Corps Song[+]; Blues in the Night; (featuring Jo Jones (drums)); Let There be Love; Love for Sale; So Beats my Heart for You;[+] Let's Face the Music and Dance (featuring Candido, Subu and Billy Exiner (drums)); Crazy rhythm; The Beat of My Heart; Lazy Afternoon (featuring Chico Hamilton (drums)); (all tracks with Ralph Sharon and his Orch.).

* July 1958

[+] On Philips BBL 7219 *only*

BBL 7280   *Long Ago and Far Away*: It Could Happen to You; Ev'ry Time we Say Goodbye; Long Ago and Far Away; It Amazes Me; The Way You Look Tonight; Be Careful, It's My Heart; My Foolish Heart; Time After Time; Fools Rush In; Cottage for Sale; So Far (w. Frank De Vol and His Orch.); Blue Moon (w. Ralph Sharon and His Orch.).

Philips: BBL 7308; CBS: BPG 62250s; S 62250s; 32373s   *In Person* (July 1959): Just in Time; When I Fall in Love; Taking a Chance on Love; Without a Song; Fascinating Rhythm; Solitude; Pennies from Heaven; Lost in the Stars; Firefly; There Will

Never Be Another You; Lullaby of Broadway; Ol' Man River (w. Count Basie and His Orch., recorded at a public performance, New York 22 December 1958).

BBL 7331 Stranger in Paradise (part side) (w. Percy Faith and his Orch. and Chorus).

BBL 7413 *To My Wonderful One*: Wonderful one; Till; September Song; Suddenly; I'm a Fool to Want You; We Mustn't Say Goodbye/Autumn Leaves; Laura; April in Paris; Speak Low; Tenderly; Last Night When We Were Young (w. Orch. dir. Frank De Vol).

BBL 7452 Alone Together; This Is All I Ask; Out of This World; Walk in the Country; I'm Always Chasing Rainbows; Poor Butterfly/After you've gone; Gone with the Wind; It's Magic; How Long Has This Been Going On; Sophisticated Lady; For Heaven's Sake (w. Orch. cond. Frank De Vol).

BBL 7455 or Stereo SBBL 609 *Tony Bennett sings Harold Arlen*: When the Sun Comes Out; Over the Rainbow; House of Flowers; Come Rain or Come Shine; For Every Man There's a Woman; Let's Fall in Love/Right as the Rain; It Was Written in the Stars; What Good Does it Do; Fun to Be Fooled; This Time the Dream's on Me; I've Got the World on a String (Orch. cond. Glenn Osser).

BBL 7479 *Tony Sings For Two*: I Didn't Know What Time it Was; Bewitched; Nobody's Heart Belongs to Me; I'm through With Love; My Funny Valentine; The Man that Got Away; Where or When; A Sleepin' Bee; Happiness Is a Thing called Joe; Mam'selle; Just Friends; Street of Dreams (w. Ralph Sharon (piano)).

BBL 7495 *My heart sings*: Don't Worry about Me; Dancing in the Dark; I'm Coming Virginia; My Heart Sings; It Never was You; You Took Advantage of Me; Close your Eyes: Stella by Starlight; More than you Know; My Ship; Lover Man; Toot, Toot, Tootsie (w. Ralph Burns and his Orch.)

BBR 8030 Cinnamon Sinner (part side) (w. Percy Faith and his Orch.)

BBR 8051 *The Voice of Your Choice*: There'll Be No Teardrops To-night[a]; Take me back Again[a]; Something's Gotta Give[b]; Stranger in Paradise[a] (w. Chorus);/Close Your Eyes[c]; What Will I Tell my Heart[a]; Tell me that you love me[a]; How Can I Replace You[a]

ᵃ w. Percy Faith and his Orch.;
ᵇ w. Orch. cond. Sid Feller;
ᶜ w. Orch. and Chorus.

BBR 8084   Come Next Spring (part side) (w. Percy Faith and his Orch.).

BBR 8089   *Cloud Seven*: I Fall in Love Too Easily; My Baby just Cares for Me; My Heart Tells Me; Old Devil Moon; Love Letters/Give Me the Simple Life; While the Music Plays On; I Can't Believe that You're in Love with Me; Darn that Dream (w. Chuck Wayne (guitar) and instrumental accomp.).

BBR 8108   Heart (part side) (w. Orch. cond. Sid Feller).

6308 157s   *Listen Easy* (July 1973): Love Is the Thing; Rain, Rain (Don't Go Away); The Hands of Time (Brian's Song); I Concentrate on You; At Long Last Love; If I Could Go Back; On the Sunny Side of the Street; Once in a Garden (The Garden of the Finzi-Continis); My Funny Valentine; How Little We Know; Tell Her that It's Snowing (w. Orch. cond. Don Costa).

6499 931s   *A Touch of Class* (Aug. 1974, reissue); Mimi (w. instrumental accomp.).

6499 932s   *A Touch of Class* (Aug. 1974, reissue): My Funny Valentine (w. Orch. cond. Don Costa).

9299 430s   *A Touch of Class* (June 1975, reissue): The End of a Love Affair (w. Orch.).

9299 431s   *A Touch of Class* (June 1975, reissue); All that Love Went to Waste (w. Orch. cond. Torrie Zito).

9299 521s   *Spotlight on Tony Bennett* (July 1975, reissue); Record 1: End of a Love Affair; Passing Strangers; All That Love Went To Waste; Love Is the Thing; On the Sunny Side of the Street; Once in a Garden; Invitation; Someone to Light up my Life; If I could Go Back; The Hands of Time; O Sole Mio; Some of These Days; The Midnight Sun; It Was You (Various Orchestras and groups/Robert Farnon, Don Costa and Torrie Zito).

9299 522s   *Spotlight on Tony Bennett,* Record 2: London by Night; My Love; Oh Lady Be Good; Cute; I Concentrate on You; Mimi; Tell Her that It's Snowing; Blues for Breakfast; At Long Last Love; My Funny Valentine; How Little We Know; Rain, Rain; The Good Things in Life; Give Me Love Give me

Peace (w. various orchestras and groups/Robert Farnon, Don Costa and Torrie Zito).

9229 524s *Words and Music* (Jan. 1976, compilation): At Long Last Love; I Concentrate on You (w. Orch. cond. Don Costa).

SON 014s *At Long Last Love* (Aug. 1976, compilation): At Long Last Love; How Little We Know; If I Could Go Back; I Concentrate on You (w. Orch. cond. Don Costa). My Love (w. Orch. cond. Torrie Zito). Someone to Light up my Life; It Was You; Passing Strangers; The End of a Love Affair; O Sole Mio; Midnight Sun; Living Together, Growing Together* (w. Orch. and *Chorus).

CBS

BPG 62116 *Tony Bennett at Carnegie Hall*: Lullaby of Broadway; Just in Time; All the Things You Are; Stranger in Paradise; Love Is Here to Stay; Climb Ev'ry Mountain; Ol' Man River; It Amazes Me; Firefly; I Left my Heart in San Francisco; How About You; April in Paris; Solitude; I'm just a Lucky So and So (w. Ralph Sharon and his Orch.).

BPG 62117 *Tony Bennett at Carnegie Hall: Part II*: Always; Anything Goes; Blue Velvet; Rags to Riches; Because of You; What Good Does it Do; Lost in the Stars; One for my Baby; Lazy Afternoon; Sing You Sinners; Love Look Away; Sometimes I'm Happy; My Heart Tells Me; De Glory Road (w. Ralph Sharon and his Orch.).

BPG 62149 *I Wanna Be Around*: Until I Met You; Let's Face the Music and Dance (w. the Ralph Sharon Trio); The Good Life; If I Love Again; I Wanna Be Around; Love Look Away; Once Upon a summertime; If you were mine; I Will Live my Life for You; Someone to Love; It Was Me; Quiet Nights (Corcovado) (w. Orch. cond. Marty Manning).

BPG 62201, 62201s, S 81226s *I Left My Heart In San Francisco*: I Left My Heart in San Francisco; Once upon a time; Tender is the Night; Smile; Love for Sale; Taking a Chance on Love; Candy Kisses; Have I Told You Lately?; Rules of the Road; Marry Young; I'm Always Chasing Rainbows; The Best Is yet to Come (w. Orch.).

BPG 62205 *This Is All I Ask*: Autumn in Rome; True Blue Lou; This Is All I ask; Got Her off my Hands; Sandy's Smile; Long about Now; Young and Foolish; On the Other Side of the Tracks (w. Chorus and Ralph Burns and his Orch.); Keep Smiling at Trouble; The Way that I Feel; The Moment of Truth (w. Ralph Burns and his Orch.); Tricks (w. Ralph Sharon Trio with Chico Hamilton (drums)).

BPG 62245 *The Many Moods of Tony*: The Little Boy; A Taste of Honey; Don't Wait too long (w Orch. cond. Dick Hyman); I'll Be Around (w. Orch. cond. Dick Hyman and Bobby Hackett (cornet)); Limehouse Blues (w. Orch. cond. Dick Hyman with Dick Hyman (organ)); When Joanna Loved Me (w. Orch. cond. Marty Manning); Soon It's Gonna Rain (w. the Ralph Sharon Trio); The Kid's a Dreamer (w. Orch. and Bobby Hackett (cornet)); So Long, Big Time! (w. Orch. cond. Harold Arlen); Caravan (w. Orch. cond. Ralph Sharon and Chico Hamilton (drums)); Spring in Manhattan (w. Orch. cond. Don Costa with The Will Bronson Singers); You've changed (w. Orch. cond. Ralph Sharon with the Noteworthies (vocal)).

BPG 62250 *In Person (With the Count Basie Orchestra)*: Just in Time; When I Fall in Love; Taking a Chance on Love; Without a Song; Fascinating Rhythm; Solitude (recorded live); Pennies from Heaven; Lost in the Stars; Firefly; There Will Never Be Another You; Lullaby of Broadway, Ol' Man River.

BPG 62296 *When Lights Are Low*: Nobody Else but Me; When Lights Are Low; On Green Dolphin Street; Ain't Misbehavin'; It's a Sin to Tell a Lie; I've Got Just about Everything; Judy; Oh! You Crazy Moon; Speak Low; It Had to be You; It Could Happen to You; The Rules of the Road (w. the Ralph Sharon Trio).

BPG 62486 *Who Can I Turn To?*: Who Can I Turn To?; Wrap Your Troubles in Dreams; There's a Lull in My Life; Autumn Leaves; I Walk a Little Faster; The Brightest Smile in Town; I've Never seen; Between the Devil and the Deep Blue Sea; Listen, Little Girl; Got the Gate on the Golden Gate; Waltz for Debbie; The Best Thing to Be is a Person (w. the Ralph Sharon Trio and with Orch. cond. George Siravo).

BPG 62544 *If I Ruled The World – Songs For The Jet Set*: Song of the jet; Fly Me to the Moon; How Insensitive; If I Ruled the World; Then Was then and Now is Now; The Right to Love;

Watch what happens (w. the Will Bronson Singers); Love Scene; My Ship; Sweet Lorraine (all w. Orch. cond. Don Costa)) All my Tomorrows) Lazy Afternoon (w. the Ralph Sharon Trio).

BPG 62677, SBPG 62677s *The Movie Song Album*: The Gentle Rain; Samba de Orfeu (w. Luiz Bonfa (guitar)); Maybe September; Emily; The Shadow of Your Smile; Smile; The Second Time Around; Days of Wine and Roses; The Trolley Song (all w. Orch. cond. Johnny Mandel); Girl Talk (w. Orch. cond. Neal Hefti); The Pawnbroker (w. Orch. cond. Quincy Jones); Never Too Late (w. Orch. cond. David Rose).

CBS BPG 62684 or Columbia OL 6550 *The Oscar* (film music): Maybe September (w. Orch. cond. Johnny Mandel).

BPG 62800 *A Time For Love*: A Time for Love; The Very Thought of You; Trapped in the Web of Love; My Funny Valentine; In the Wee Small Hours; Yesterdays; Georgia Rose; The Shining Sea; Sleepy Time Gal; Touch the Earth; I'll Only Miss Her When I Think of Her (w. the Ralph Sharon Trio and Orchestras cond. by Ralph Sharon, Johnny Keating, Johnny Mandel and Ralph Burns).

BPG 62821 *Tony's Greatest Hits*: I Left My Heart in San Francisco; I Wanna be Around; Corcovado; When Joanna loved me; The Good Life; Once Upon a Time (w. Ralph Sharon (piano) and Orch. cond. Marty Manning); The Moment of Truth; This Is All I Ask (w. Orch. cond. Ralph Burns); Who Can I Turn To? (w. Orch. cond. George Siravo); A Taste of Honey (w. Orch. cond. Dick Hyman); The Best Is yet to Come (w. Orch. cond. Cy Coleman); If I Ruled the World (w. the Will Bronson Singers and Orch. cond. Don Costa).

BPG 63055 *Tony Bennett Makes it Happen*: On the Sunny Side of the Street; A Beautiful kind of Friendship; Don't Get around Much Anymore; What Makes It Happen; The Lady's in Love with You; Can't get out of this Mood; I Don't Know Why; I Let a Song Go Out of My Heart; Country Girl; Old Devil Moon; She's Funny That Way (w. Marion Evans and his Orch.).

BPG 63166 or SBPG 63166s *For Once in My Life*: They Can't Take That Away from Me; Something in your Smile; Days of

Love; Broadway; Crazy Rhythm; Lullaby of Broadway; For once in my Life; Sometimes I'm Happy; Out of This World; Baby, Dream your Dream; How do You Say Auf Wiedersehen; Keep Smiling at Trouble (w. John Bunch and Lou Levy (piano), Bobby Tricarico (saxophone), Burt Collins (flugelhorn) and Orchestras cond. by Marion Evans, Torrie Zito, David Rose and Ralph Burns).

S 63351s *Yesterday I Heard the Rain*: Yesterday I Heard the Rain; Hi-ho; Hushabye Mountain; Home Is the Place; Love is Here to Stay; Get Happy; Fool of Fools; I Only Have Eyes for You; Sweet Georgie Fame; Only the Young; There Will Never Be Another You (w. Orch.).

63612s *Tony Bennett's Greatest Hits – Volume II*: People; For Once in my Life; Shadow of Your Smile; Yesterday I Heard the Rain; Georgia Rose; A Time for Love (w. Orchestras cond. by Torri Zito, Johnny Mandel, and Ralph Burns); Watch What Happens; How Insensitive; Fly Me to the Moon (w. the Will Bronson Singers and Orch. cond. Don Costa); My Favourite things (w. Dave Carey (vibraphone) and Orch. cond. Robert Farnon); The Gentle Rain (w. Luiz Bonfa (guitar) and Orch. cond. Johnny Mandel).

S 63685s *I've gotta be me*: Over the sun (w. Gene Bertocini (guitar)); Play it again, Sam (w. Marky Markowitz (trumpet)); Alfie; What the world needs now is love; Baby, don't you quit now; That night; They all laughed; A lonely place; Whoever you are, I love you; Valley of the Dolls (all with Orch. cond. Torrie Zito).

63782s *Snowfall – The Tony Bennett Christmas Album*: We Wish You a Merry Christmas; Silent Night, Holy Night; Adeste Fideles (O come, all ye faithful); Jingle bells; Where is Love (w. Choir); Snowfall; My Favourite Things; The Christmas Song; Santa Claus is Comin' to Town; Christland; I've Got my Love to Keep me Warm; White Christmas; Winter Wonderland; Have Yourself a Merry Little Christmas; I love the Winter Weather (w. Orch. cond. Robert Farnon).

63962s, S 81227s *Tony sings the Great Hits of Today*: MacArthur Park; Something; The Look of Love; Here, There and Everywhere; Vivre Pour Vivre (Live for Life); Little Green Apples; Eleanor Rigby; My Cherie Amour; Is that All There is?; Here;

Sunrise, Sunset (w. Orch.).

S 64200s *Tony Bennett sings his All-time Hall of Fame Hits*: Because of You; Rags to Riches; I Left my Heart in San Francisco; I wanna be around; This is All I Ask; The Shadow of Your Smile; Who Can I Turn To?; Yesterday I Heard the Rain; For Once in My Life (w. Orch. cond. by Percy Faith, Marty Manning, Ralph Burns, Johnny Mandel, George Siravo and Torrie Zivo); Cold, Cold Heart; One for My Baby/ It Had to Be You; The Good Life (w. John Bunch (piano)). (With spoken introductions by Tony Bennett).

S 64217s *Tony Bennett's Something*: Something; The Long and Winding Road; Everybody's Talking; On a Clear Day You Can See Forever (from the musical); Coco (from the musical); Think How It's Gonna Be (from the musical *Applause*); Wave; Make it Easy on Yourself; Come Saturday Morning (from the film *Pookie*); When I Look in Your Eyes (from the film *Doctor Dolittle*); Se te Olvida (Yellow days); What a Wonderful World (w. Orch. cond. Peter Katz).

S 64368s *Love Story*: Love Story (Where Do I Begin); Tea for Two; I Want to be Happy; Individual Thing (from the Musical *Prettybelle*); I Do not Know a Day I Did not Love You (from the musical *Two by two*); They Can't Take that Away from Me; When Joanna Loved Me; Country Girl; The Gentle Rain*; Soon It's Gonna Rain; A Taste of Honey; I'll Begin Again (w. Orch.). (w. Luis Bonfa (guitar)*.

S 64443s *Love Songs*: Alone Together; The Very Thought of You; Tender is the Night; I Only Have Eyes for You; Laura; When We're Alone (Penthouse Serenade); Stella by Starlight (w. Orch.); Bewitched; Where or when; Street of dreams (w. piano accomp.).

S 64444s *Love Songs*: Tenderly; September Song; Days of Wine and Roses; I Cover the Waterfront; The Second Time Around; Till; Love for Sale (w. Orch.); It Had to be You; My Funny Valentine (w. piano and rhythm accomp.); I'm Through with Love (with piano).

S 64577s *Get Happy with the London Philharmonic*: I Want to Be Happy; If I Ruled the World; Get Happy; Tea for Two; Let There be Love; Love Story; The Trolley Song; Medley:– I Left my Heart in San Francisco/I Wanna Be Around; Old Devil

160

Moon; Country Girl; There Will Never Be Another You; Wave; On the Sunny Side of the Street; For Once in My Life; What the World Needs Now is Love; I'll Begin Again (w. the London Philharmonic Orch. cond. Robert Farnon).

S 64848s *Summer of Forty-two*: The Summer knows; Walk-about; It Was Me; I'm Losing My Mind; Till; Somewhere Along the Line; Coffee Break; More and More; Irina; My Inamorata; The Shining Sea (w. Orch.).

s 64849s *With Love*: Here's that Rainy Day; Remind Me; The Riviera; Street of Dreams; Love; Twilight World; How Beautiful is Night (With You); Lazy Day in Love; Easy Come, Easy Go; Harlem Butterfly; Dream (w. Robert Farnon and his Orch. and John Bunch (piano)).

S 65282s *Tony Bennett's All-Time Greatest Hits*, Record 1: Something; (Where Do I Begin) Love Story; Maybe This Time; Just in Time; For Once in My Life; Firefly; The Shadow Of Your Smile; Put on a Happy Face; Love Look Away; Rags to Riches (w. Orch.).

S 65283s *Tony Bennett's All-Time Greatest Hits,* Record 2: A Time for Love; Who Can I Turn To; That Is All I Ask; Smile; Sing You Sinners; I Left My Heart in San Francisco; Because of You; Boulevard of Broken Dreams; Stanger in Paradise; I Wanna Be Around (w. Orchestra).

DP 66010, SDP 66010s *A String of Tony's Hits*, Record 1: Stranger in Paradise; Cold, Cold heart; Because of You; Rags to Riches; Boulevard of Broken Dreams; Young Warm and Wonderful; In the Middle of an Island; Ça, C'est l'Amour; Just in Time; There'll Be No Teardrops Tonight; Anywhere I Wander; Sing you sinners (w. Chorus and Orch.).

DP 66010, SDP 66010s *A String of Tony's Hits*, Record 2: Smile; You'll Never Get away from Me; I Am; Put on a Happy Face; Love Look Away; I'll bring You a Rainbow; Ask Anyone in Love; You Can't Love 'em All; Baby Talk to Me; Firefly.

66205B *CBS Showcase*, Record 11: A Taste of Honey (w. Orch cond. Dick Hyman).

66297 *Love Songs* (2 LP set): Alone Together; Bewitched; Very Thought of You; Tender Is the Night; I Only Have Eyes for You; Tenderly; I'm Through with Love; September Song; My Funny Valentine; Days of Wine and Roses; Where or When;

161

Laura; Penthouse Serenade; Street of Dreams; Stella by Starlight; I Cover the Waterfront; Second Time Around; It Had to be You; Till; Love for Sale.

S 70115s   *The Last Picture Show* (film soundtrack): Cold, Cold Heart; Blue Velvet; Solitaire (w. Orch.).

S 80796s   *Let's Fall in Love with the Songs of Harold Arlen* (July 1975, reissue): When the Sun Comes Out; House of Flowers; Come Rain or Come Shine; Let's Fall in Love; Over the Rainbow; Right as the Rain; It was Written in the Stars; Fun to be Fooled; This Time the Dream's on Me; I've Got the World on a String (w. Orch. cond. Glen Osser).

S 80797s   *Let's Fall in Love with the Songs of Cy Coleman* (July 1975, reissue): I've Got Your Number; On the Other Side of the Tracks; Firefly; The Rules of the Road; The Riviera; The Best is Yet to Come; I Walk a Little Faster; It Amazes Me; Baby, Dream Your Dream; Then Was Then and Now is Now (with various orchestras and conductors).

81226/27   *I Left My Heart in San Francisco/Tony Sings the Great Hits of Today*

88131   *Let's Fall in Love with the Songs of Arlen and Coleman*: When the Sun Comes Out; House of Flowers; Come Rain Come Shine; Let's Fall in Love; Over the Rainbow; Right as the Rain; It Was Written in the Stars; Fun to be Fooled; This Time the Dream is on Me; I've Got the World on a String; I've Got Your Number; On the Other Side of the Tracks; Firefly; The Riviera; The Best Is yet to Come; I Walk a Little Faster; It Amazes Me; Baby Dream Your Dream; Then Was Then and Now Is Now.

32373/40-32373 *In Person (With Count Basie)* (re-issued Autumn 1983).

MGM/Philips

MGM MV 5088s, Philips 6308 134s   *The Good Things in Life*: The Good Things in Life; O sole Mio; Passing Strangers; End of a Love Affair; Oh, Lady Be Good; Blues for Breakfast; Mimi; Invitation; Someone to Light up My Life; It was You; Cute; The Midnight Sun; London by Night; The Good Things in Life (reprise) (w. Orch. arranged and cond. Robert Farnon; John Bunch (piano); Kenny Clare (drums); Arthur Watts (bass).

10.

Repackaged and Reissued Material

The following release listing is mainly repackaged and reissued material. Of course some of the preceding albums are of this sort but since they were issued on Philips, the last major company to issue new Bennett material, they have been left to run on from the other material. The listing order from the first Allegro album follows in an alphabetical order.

Allegro
ALLR 799 *One Night Stand*: Strike up the Band; I Guess I'll Have to Change My Plans; Chicago; Growing Pains; Life Is a Song; I've Grown Accustomed to Her Face; Jeepers Creepers; Anything Goes; Poor Little Rich Girl; Are You Havin' any Fun (w. Count Basie and his Orch.).

CBS
WSR 851 *Command Performance*: Tony's track is 'If I Ruled the World', with the Will Bronson Chorus and Orch. cond. Don Costa.

CBS (Embassy)
S 31524s *Best Of the 60s* (May 1978, compilation): I left my heart in San Francisco (w. Orch. cond. Marty Manning).

CBS
S 31606(s) *Season's Best* (Dec. 1977, compilation): The Christmas Song (w. Orch. cond. Robert Farnon)
32373 *In Person (With Count Basie and his Orch.)* (Sept. 1983)

Columbia
SEG 7981 *Tony Bennett*: Chicago; With Plenty of Money and You; Jeepers Creepers; Poor Little Rich Girl; Are You Havin'

any Fun (w. Count Basie and his Orch. *recorded* New York, 19 November 1958).

Columbia 33SX 1174, Saga Eros 8076s, Jazz Reactivation JR 149s* *Basie/Bennett* (July 1982*, reissue*): Life Is a Song; With Plenty of Money and You; Jeepers Creepers; Are You Havin' any Fun; Anything Goes; Strike up the Band; Chicago; I've Grown Accustomed to her Face; Poor Little Rich Girl; Growing Pains; I Guess I'll Have to Change my Plans (*with* Count Basie and His Orch. *recorded* New York, 19 November 1958).

Concord Jazz

CJ-50s *A Tribute To Duke*: Prelude to a Kiss; I'm Just a Lucky So and So; (w. Nat Pierce (piano), Scott Hamilton (tenor sax), Bill Berry (trumpet), Monty Budwig (bass), Jake Hanna (drums); recorded Hollywood, published 1977).

Contour

6870 662s *Ah! Men* (October 1975, compilation): My Funny Valentine (w. Orch. cond. Don Costa).

Decca

LK 4903; SKL 4903s *Ted Heath 21st Anniversary Album* (speaking); Tribute to Ted Heath.

Embassy

EMB 31002s *The Trolley Song* (Nov. 1973, reissues): The Trolley Song; Days of Wine and Roses; Girl Talk; I've Gotta Be Me; Alfie; What the World Needs Now; Old Devil Moon; She's Funny that Way; On the Sunny Side of the Street; A Beautiful Friendship; There Will Never Be Another You; Fascinatin' Rhythm (w. Orch.).

EMB 31058s *If I Ruled the World* (Sept. 1974, reissues): Song of the Jet; Fly Me to the Moon; How Insensitive; If I Ruled the World; Then Was Then and Now Is Now; The Right to Love; Watch What Happens (w. the Will Bronson Singers and Orch. cond. Don Costa); Love scene; Sweet Lorraine (w. Orch. cond. Don Costa); All my Tomorrows (w. the Ralph Sharon Trio); Take the Moment; Two by Two (w. Chorus and Orch.).

EMB 31078s *Million Sellers of the Fifties*: Rags to Riches (w.

Percy Faith and his Orch.); Stranger in Paradise (w. Percy Faith and his Orch. and Chorus).

EMB 31252s   *Great Film Hits* (Apr. 1976): The Summer Knows (from *Summer of '42*) (w. Orch.); A Taste of Honey (from the film) (w. Orch cond. Dick Hyman).

EMB 31253s   *Best of the 60s* (Apr. 1976, compilation): I Left My Heart In San Francisco (w. Orch.).

Fantasy

FT 527s   *Tony Bennett/Bill Evans Album* (March 1976): Young and Foolish; The Touch of Your Lips; Some Other Time; When in Rome; We'll Be Together Again; My Foolish Heart; Waltz for Debbie; But Beautiful; The Days of Wine and Roses (w. Bill Evans (piano)).

Golden Hour

GH 869s   *Golden Hour Of Tony Bennett, Sarah Vaughan And Count Basie* (Jan. 1978, compilation): Strike Up the Band; I've Grown Accustomed to Her Face; Life Is a Song; Chicago; Anything Goes; With Plenty of Money and You; Jeepers Creepers; Are You Havin' any Fun?; Poor Little Rich Girl; Growing Pains; I Guess I'll Have to Change my Plan (w. Count Basie and his Orch., all recorded c. 1959).

Hallmark

SHM 646s   *Just One of Those Things*: Let's Begin; Just One of Those Things (w. Art Blakey (drums) and Ralph Sharon Orch.); Lullaby of Broadway; Blues in the Night (w. Jo Jones (drums) and Ralph Sharon Orch.); Let There be Love; Love for Sale; Let's Face the Music and Dance (w. Candido, Sabu, Billy Exiner (drums) and Ralph Sharon Orch.); Crazy rhythm; Beat of my Heart; Lazy Afternoon (with Chico Hamilton (drums) and Ralph Sharon Orch.).

SHM 769s   *The Very Thought of You*: Just in Time; Don't Get Around Much Anymore; The Very Thought of You; Stranger in Paradise; The Second Time Around; Stella by Starlight; It's Magic; Laura; If I Love Again; I'll Be Around; (w. Orchestras cond. by Ralph Sharon, Marion Evans, Johnny Keating, Johnny Mandel, Frank de Vol, Marty Manning and Dick Hyman).

165

SHM 817s *When I Fall in Love* (Feb. 1974, reissues): April in Paris; Solitude; How about You; Old Man River; Firefly (recorded at Carnegie Hall w. Ralph Sharon and his Orch.); Pennies from Heaven; When I fall in love; Taking a Chance on Love (recorded at a public performance w. Count Basie and his Orch.); Country Girl; They All Laughed; The Gentle Rain; Play It Again Sam (w. Orch.).

Improv

7112s *Life Is Beautiful*: Life Is Beautiful; All Mine; Bridges; Reflections; Experiment; This Funny World; As Time Goes By; I Used to be Color Blind; Lost in the Stars; There'll Be Some Changes Made (w. Orch. cond. Torrie Zito).

IMP 7113s *(Ten) Rodgers and Hart Songs* (Dec. 1976): This Can't Be Love; Blue Moon; The Lady Is a Tramp; Lover; Manhattan; Spring is Here; Have You Met Miss Jones?; Isn't it Romantic?; Wait 'Til You See Her; I Could Write a Book (w. the Ruby Braff–George Barnes Quartet: Ruby Braff (cornet), George Barnes (guitar), Wayne Wright (guitar), John Giuffrida (bass)).

K-TEL

NE 490s *20 All Time Greats of the '50s*: Young and Warm and Wonderful (w. Frank De Vol and his Orch.).

NE 491s *20 Everlasting Memories of the '50s* (Aug. 1974, reissues): I Left my Heart in San Francisco (w. Orch. cond. Marty Manning).

London Palladium

RVP 252s *25 Years of Royal Variety at the London Palladium* (Dec. 1973): I left my heart in San Francisco (w. Orch.). (Original 1972 recording, introduced by Max Bygraves).

Lotus

WH 5002s *Moments to Remember* (Oct. 1978, compilation): I left my heart in San Francisco (w. Orch. cond. Marty Manning) (Pub. c. 1962.)

Ronco

MSD 2005s *Command Performance* (Dec. 1973): I left my heart in San Francisco (w. Orch. recorded live on Ed Sullivan TV Show).

P 11772s *A Christmas Present* (compilation): The Christmas Song (w. Orch. cond. Robert Farnon).

P 12430s *A Christmas Gift* (Dec. 1975, compilation): Santa Claus is Coming to Town (w. instrumental accomp. and strings).

RTL 2062s *Memories Are Made of This* (Nov. 1981, compilation): Stranger in Paradise (w. Percy Faith and his Orch. and Chorus (℗ 1955)).

RTL 2062s *Memories Are Made of This* (Nov. 1981): (w. Percy Faith and his Orch).

Roulette

2934 003s *Summit Meeting*: Chicago; Poor Little Rich Girl; I Guess I'll Have to Change my Plan; Life Is a Song; With Plenty of Money and You; Jeepers Creepers; Are You Having Any Fun; Anything Goes; Strike up the Band (w. Count Basie and his Orch.).

Saga

EROS 8138s I've grown accustomed to her face; Anything goes (w. Count Basie and his Orch.).

St Michael

M 0501211s *Moods For Lovers* (Feb. 1979, compilation): Love for Sale; MacArthur Park (w. Orch.)

Save the Children Fund

6830034s *Stars Sing a Rainbow*: In other words (w. the Will Bronson Singers and Orch. cond. Don Costa).

Telstar

Star 2230s *20 Great Italian Love Songs* (Apr. 1983, compilation): Autumn in Rome;* Begin the beguine (with Chorus and Orch. accomp.; *℗ 1963).

Warwick

PR 5021s *The Very Best of Tony Bennett* (April 1977, compilation): I Left my Heart in San Francisco; I Wanna be Around; When Joanna Loved Me; Who Can I Turn To; The Good Life; A Taste of Honey; If I Ruled the World; What the World Needs Now; Fascinatin' Rhythm; Taking a Chance on Love; Candy Kisses; Something; Just in time; Firefly; Put on a Happy Face; Stranger in Paradise; People; For Once in my Life; The Shadow of Your Smile; My Favourite Things (recorded 1957–70).

WW 5046s *Love Songs* (Nov. 1978, compilation): The Shadow of Your Smile (w. Orch. cond. Johnny Madel). (Pub. c. 1966).

11.

A to Z of Song Titles

Singles, EPs

Record code: DB = Columbia; PB = Philips; BBE = Philips
AAG is CBS, as is AGG.

Afraid of the Dark   PB 537
After You've Gone   BBE 12461
All That Love Went to Waste (from the film *A Touch of Class*)   6006 372
Alone Together   BBE 12461
Anywhere I Wander   Columbia DB 3198
Ask Anyone in Love   PB 1079; BBE 12424 (EP)
Ask Me (I Know)   PB 1008
Baby Dream Your Dream   CBS 2970
Baby Talk Me   PB 1149
Because of You   Columbia DB 2924
Being True to One Another   PB 907
Best Is Yet to Come, The   PB 1218
Blue Velvet   CBS ACG 20037; DB 2972
Boulevard of Broken Dreams   BBE 12223
Ça, C'est l'Amour   PB 753; BBE 12159 (EP)
Can You Find It in Your Heart   PB 501
Capri May   PB 563
Cinnamon Sinner   PB 322
Caravan   CBS AGG 20052 (EP)
Climb Every Mountain   PB 1122; BBE 12437 (EP, part side)
Cold Cold Heart   Columbia DB 2924
Cool School   PB 996
Come Next Spring   PB 537

Congratulations to Someone   DB 3925; SCM 5048
Corcovado (Quiet Night)   AAG 225
Country Girl   CBS 2970
Days of Love   CBS 2779
Don't Tell Me Why   PB 486
Don't Wait Too Long   AAG 126
Easy Come, Easy Go   7984
Eleanor Rigby   5255
Firefly   PB 855; BBE 12223 (EP)
Follow Me   AAG 208
Fool of Fools, A   CBS 3370
For Once in My Life   CBS 3064
Forget Me Not   PB 501
From the Candy Store on the Corner to the Chapel on the
   Hill   PB 628
Funny Thing   PB 390
Georgia Rose   CBS 202346
Give Me Love (Give Me Peace on Earth)   6006326
Glory of Love, The   CBS 3370
Good Life, The   AAG 153; AGG 20037
Good Things in Life, The   Philips 6006 309
Good Times in Life, The   CBS 6006 260
Happiness Street   PB 628
Have a Good Time   DB 3178
Heart   PB 672
Here Comes that Heartache Again   PB 267
Hi-Ho   CBS 3731
How Beautiful is the Night   7535
How Can I Replace You?   PB 421
How Do You Say Auf Wiedersehen?   CBS 3064
How Long Has This Been Going On?   Philips BBE 12461
Hushabye Mountain   CBS 3731
I Am   PB 724
I Can't Give You Anything but Love   Columbia DB 2988
I Fall in Love Too Easily   BBE 12273 (EP)
I Left my Heart in San Francisco   CBS 1143 (Hall of Fame
   series); 6151 (EP); AAG 121; 201730
I Lose Your Eyes   PB 445
I Never Felt More like Falling in Love   PB 786

I Wanna be Around   AAG 137; 201733
I Want to be Happy   CBS 7342
I Will Live my Life for You   AAG 1371; CBS 201733
I Won't Cry Anymore   Columbia DB 2972
I've Gotta be Me   CBS 4527
If I Ruled the World   CBS 201735; (EP) 6151
I'll Begin Again   CBS 5307
I'll Bring You a Rainbow   PB 1008
My Love   Philips 6006 326
In Other Words (Fly Me to the Moon)   CBS 6066 (EP)
In the Middle of an Island   BBE 12415, Philips 12159 (EP);
   PB 724
It Had to be You   BBE 12223
It's so Beautiful in the Country   PB 907
It's too Soon to Know   PB 445
Just in Time   BBE 12148 (part side); BBE 12148 (EP); BBE
   12159; PB 735
Just Say I Love Her   Columbia DB 2789
Keep Smiling at Trouble   CBS 2779
The Kid's a Dreamer   AAG 191
Kisses I'll never Forget   PB 477
Limehouse Blues   AAG 176
Little Boy, The   AAG 184
Little Green Apples   CBS 4986
Living Together, Growing Together   Philips 6006 260
Lonely Place, A   CBS 4527
Love Is the Thing   Philips 6006 309
Love Look Away   PB 996
Love Me, Love Me, Love Me   PB 786
Marriage-Go-Round   PB 1089; BBE 12424 (EP)
Marry Young   AAG 126
Maybe This Time   CBS 8095
May I Never Love Again   PB 486; BBE 12009 (EP)
MacArthur Park   CBS 5255
Moment of Truth, The   AAG 20052 (EP); AAG 184
More and More   CBS 8095; CBS 7342
Night that Heaven Fell   PB 855
No Hard Feelings   PB 710
No One Will Ever Know   PB 216

Not as a Stranger   PB 357
Now I Lay Me Down to Sleep   PB 831
Madonna, Madonna   PB 357
One for My Baby   PB 720; BBE 12159 (EP)
One Kiss away from Heaven   PB 689
Our Lady of Fatima   Columbia DB 2789
Penthouse Serenade   BBE 12338
Please Driver   PB 390
My Cherie Amour   CBS 5307
People   CBS 4092
Play It Again Sam   CBS 4224
Punch and Judy Love   BBE 12009 (EP); PB 477
Put on a Happy Face   PB 149
Quiet Nights   AGG 20037
Rags to Riches   PB 216
Ramona   PB 1122
Second Time Around   CBS 202084
September Song   EP 6071
Since my Love Has Gone   DB 3101
Sing You Sinners   PB 563
Shadow of Your Smile   CBS 202084
Skyscraper Blues, The   BBE 12338
Sleepy Time Gal   CBS 202021
Smile   PB 961
So Long, Big Time   AGG 20052 (EP)
Sold to the Man with the Broken Heart   PB 689
Some of These Days   Philips 6006 372
Somebody   PB 1089; BBE 12424 (EP)
Something   CBS 4958
Somewhere along the Line   CBS 7711
Somewhere along the Way   DB 3101
Soon It's Gonna Rain   AAG 208
Speak Low   CBS 6071 (EP)
Spring in Manhattan   AAG 153
Stay Where You Are   DB 3918
Stranger in Paradise   BBE 12009 (EP), PB 420
Summer Knows, The   7711
Sweet Georgie Fame   CBS 3573
Take Me   DB 3295; SCM 5048

Take Me Back Again   BBE 12009 (EP); PB 420
Taste of Honey, A   CBS (EP) 6066
Tea for Two   CBS 7056
Tell Me that You Love Me   PB 521
Tender Is the Night   PB 1218
There'll Be No Teardrops Tonight   PB 267
They All Laughed   CBS 4092
This Is All I Asked   CBS 6066 (EP); AAG 165; BBE 12461
Till   CBS 6071 (EP); PB 1079
Time for Love, A   202346
True Blue Love   AAG 165
Twilight World   CBS 7984
Until I Met You   AAG 20037
Until Yesterday   PB 322
Very Thought of You, The   CBS 6151; CBS 202021
Walkabout (theme from the film)   CBS 7535
We Mustn't Say Goodbye   CBS 6071
What the World Needs Now Is Love   CBS 4224
Whatever Lola Wants   PB 672
When Joanna Loved Me   CBS 6066 (EP); AAG 191
Where Do I Begin? (theme from *Love Story*)   CBS 7056
While We're Young   DB 2988
Who Can I Turn To?   CBS 201735; CBS 6151 (EP); AAG 225
Yesterday I Heard the Rain (Esta Tarde Vi Llover)   CBS 3370
You Can't Love 'em All   PB 961
You could Make Me Smile Again   DB 3178
You'll Never Get Away from Me   AAG 126
Young and Foolish   AGG 20052 (EP)
Young Warm and Wonderful   PB 831

A to Z of Song Titles: LPs

Song titles from LPs and their source(s) are listed. BBR, BBL are
prefixes of Philips.
Adeste Fideles (O Come All Ye Faithful)   *Snowfall: The Tony
   Bennett Christmas Album* (CBS 637825)
After You've Gone   *Tony Bennett* (BBL 7452)
Ain't Misbehavin'   *When Lights Are Low* (CBS BPG 62296)

Alfie *I've Gotta Be Me* (CBS 63685)

Always *Tony Bennett at Carnegie Hall*, Part 2 (CBS BPG 62117), *Tony Bennett Showcase* (BBL 7138)

All My Tomorrows *If I Ruled the World – Songs for the Jet Set* (CBS BPG 62544)

All that Love Went to Waste *Spotlight on Tony Bennett*, Record 1 (Philips 9299521); *A Touch of Class* (PL 9299 431)

All the Things You Are *Tony Bennett at Carnegie Hall* (CBS BPG 62116)

Alone Together *Tony Bennett* (BBL 7452); *Love Songs* (CBS 6443); *Love Songs* (CBS 66297)

Ask Anyone in Love *A String of Tony's Hits*, Record 2 (CBS DP 66010)

Anywhere I Wander *A String of Tony's Hits* (CBS DP 66010)

Anything Goes *Tony Bennett at Carnegie Hall*, Pt. 2 (CBS BPG 62117)

April in Paris *To My Wonderful One* (BBL 7413); *Tony Bennett at Carnegie Hall* (CBS BPG 62116)

Army Air Corps Song *The Beat of My Heart* (BBL 7219)

At Long Last Love *Listen Easy* (Philips 6308157); *Spotlight on Tony Bennett*, Record 2 (Philips 92919 521); *Words and Music* (Philips 9299 524); *At Long Last Love* (Philips SON 014)

Autumn in Rome *This Is All I Ask* (CBS BPG 62205)

Autumn Leaves *To My Wonderful One* (BBL 7413); *Who Can I Turn To?* (CBS BPG 62486)

Baby Don't You Quit Now *I've Gotta Be Me* (CBS 636855)

Baby Dream Your Dream *For Once in My Life* (CBS BPG 63166); *Let's Fall in Love to the Songs of Cy Coleman* (CBS 80797)

Baby Talk To Me *A String of Tony's Hits*, Record 2 (CBS DP 66010)

Beautiful Kind of Friendship, A *Tony Bennett Makes It Happen* (CBS BPG 63055)

Be Careful, It's My Heart *Long Ago and Far Away* (BBL 7280)

Because of You *Tony Bennett at Carnegie Hall*, Pt. 2 (CBS BPG 62117); *Tony Bennett Sings His All-Time Hall of Fame Hits* (CBS 64200); *Tony Bennett All-Time Greatest Hits*, Record 2 (CBS 65283); *A String of Tony's Hits*, Record 1 (CBS DP 66010)

Best Is Yet to Come, The *I Left My Heart in San Francisco* (CBS BPG 62201); *Tony's Greatest Hits* (CBS BPG 62821); *Let's*

Fall in Love to the Songs of Cy Coleman (CBS 80797)

Best Thing Is to Be a Person, The   *Who Can I Turn To?* (CBS 62486)

Bewitched   *Two Songs for Two* (BBL 7479); *Love Songs* (CBS 64443); *Love Songs* (66297)

Blue Velvet   *Tony Bennett at Carnegie Hall,* 11 (CBS BPG 62117); *The Last Picture Box* (CBS 70115)

Blues for Breakfast   *The Good Things in Life* (MGM MV 5088, Philips 6308134); *Spotlight on Tony Bennett,* vol. 2 (Philips 9299522)

Blues in the Night   *The Beat of my Heart/Just One of those Things* (Harmony HS 11340)

Boulevard of Broken Dreams   *Tony Bennett Showcase* (BBL 7138); *Tony Bennett's All-Time Greatest Hits,* Record 2 (65283); *A String of Tony's Hits* (CBSDP 66010)

Brightest Smile in Town, The   *Who Can I Turn To?* (CBS BPG 62486)

Broadway   *For Once in My Life* (CBS SBPG 63166)

Ça, C'est l'Amour   *A String of Tony's Hits* (CBS DP 66010)

Candy Kisses   *I Left My Heart in San Francisco* (CBS BPG 62201)

Can't Get Out of This Mood   *Tony Bennett Makes It Happen* (CBS BPG 63055)

Christland   *Tony Bennett Christmas Album* (CBS 637828)

Christmas Song, The   *Snowfall – The Tony Bennett Christmas Album* (CBS 63782)

Climb Every Mountain   *Tony Bennett at Carnegie Hall* (CBS BPG 62116)

Close Your Eyes   *My Heart Sings* (BBL 7495); *The Voice of Your Choice* (BBR 8051)

Coco (from the musical)   *Tony Bennett's Something* (CBS 64217)

Coffee Break   *Summer of Forty Two* (CBS 64848)

Cold Cold Heart   *Tony Bennett Sings His All-Time Hall of Fame Hits* (CBS 64200); *A String of Tony's Hits,* Record 1 (CBS DP 66010); *The Last Picture Box* (CBS 70155)

Come Rain or Come Shine   *Tony Bennett Sings Harold Arlen* (BBL 7455, BBL 609); *Let's Fall in Love with the Songs of Harold Arlen* (CBS 80796)

Come Saturday Morning   *Tony Bennett Sings Something* (CBS 5624217)

Cottage for Sale   *Long Ago and Far Away* (BBL 7280)

Country Girl   *Tony Bennett Makes It Happen* (CBS BPG 63055); *Love Story* (CBS 64368); *Get Happy* with the London Philharmonic (CBS 64577)

Crazy Rhythm   *The Beat of My Heart* (BBL 7219); *Just One of Those Things* (Harmony HS 11340); *For Once in My Life* (BPG 63166)

Cute   *The Good Things in Life* (MGM 5088, Philips 6308134); *Spotlight on Tony Bennett*, Record 2 (9299522)

Dancing in the Dark   *My Heart Sings* (BBL 7495)

Darn that Dream   *Cloud Seven* (BBR 8089)

Days of Love   *For Once in My Life* (CBS BPG 63166)

Days of Wine and Roses *Love Songs* (CBS 64444/66297); *The Movie Album* (CBS BPG 62677); *Love Songs* (CBS 64444)

De Glory Road   *Tony Bennett at Carnegie Hall* (CBS BPG 62117)

Don't Get Around Much Anymore   *Tony Bennett Makes It Happen* (CBS BPG 63055)

Don't Wait Too Long   *The Many Moods of Tony* (CBS BPG 62245)

Don't Worry About Me   *My Heart Sings* (BBL 7495)

Dream   *In Love* (CBS 64849)

Easy Come, Easy Go   *With Love* (CBS 64849)

Eleanor Rigby   *Tony Sings the Great Hits of Today* (CBS 63962/81227)

Emily   *The Movie Song Album* (CBS BPG 62677)

End of a Love Affair, The   *The Good Things in Life* (MGM 5088, Philips 6308 134); *Spotlight on Tony Bennett*, Record 1 (Philips 9249 521); *A Touch of Class* (Philips 9299 430); *At Long Last Love* (Philips SON 014)

Everybody's Talking   *Tony Bennett's Something* (CBS 64217)

Every Time We Say Goodbye   *Long Ago and Far Away* (BBL 7280)

Fascinating Rhythm   *In Person* (BBL 7308, CBS BPG 62250, 32373); *In Person* (CBS BPG 62250)

Firefly   *In Person* (BBL 7308, CBS BPG 62250, 32373); *Tony Bennett at Carnegie Hall* (CBS BPG 62116); *In Person* (CBS BPG 62250); *Tony Bennett's All-Time Greatest Hits* (CBS 65250); *A string of Tony's Hits* (CBS DP 66010); *Let's Fall in Love with the Songs of Cy Coleman* (CBS 80797)

Fly Me to the Moon   *If I Ruled the World – Songs for the Jet Set* (CBS BPG 62544); *Tony Bennett's Greatest Hits*, Vol. 2 (63125)

Fool of Fools   *Yesterday I Heard the Rain* (CBS 63351)

Fools Rush In   *Long Ago and Far Away* (BBL 7280)

For Every Man There's a Woman   *Tony Bennett Sings Harold Arlen* (BBL 7455, BBL 609)

For Heaven's Sake   *Tony Bennett* (BBL 7452)

For Once in My Life   *For Once in My Life* (CBS BPG 63166); *Tony Bennett's Greatest Hits*, Volume 2 (CBS 636128); *Tony Bennett Sings His All-Time Hall of Fame Hits* (CBS 64200); *Get Happy, with the London Philharmonic* (CBS 63577); *Tony Bennett's All-Time Greatest Hits* (CBS 65282)

Fun To Be Fooled *Let's Fall in Love with the Songs of Harold Arlen* (CBS 80796)

Fun To Be Fooled   *Tony Bennett Sings Harold Arlen* (BBL 7455, BBL 609)

Georgie Rose   *A Time for Love* (CBS BPG 62800); *Tony Bennett's Greatest Hits*, Vol. 2 (CBS 63628)

Gentle Rain, The   *The Movie Song Album* (CBS BPG 62677); *Tony Bennett's Greatest Hits, Vol. 2* (CBS 63612); *Love Story* (CBS 643688)

Get Happy   *Yesterday I Heard the Rain* (CBS 63351); *Get Happy with the London Philharmonic* (64577)

Girl Talk   *The Movie Song Album* (CBS BPG 62677)

Give Me Love Give Me Peace   *Spotlight on Tony Bennett, Record 2* (Philips 9299522)

Give Me the Simple Life   *Cloud Seven* (BBR 8089)

Gone with the Wind   *Tony Bennett* (BBL 7452)

Good Life, The   *I Wanna Be Around* (CBS BPG 62149); *Tony's Greatest Hits* (BPG 62821)

Good Things in Life   *The Good Things in Life* (MGM 5088, Philips 6308 134); *Spotlight on Tony Bennett*, Vol. 1 (Philips 9299522)

Got Her off My Hands   *This Is All I Ask* (CBS BPG 62205)

Got the Gate on the Golden Gate   *Who Can I Turn To?* (CBS BPG 62486)

Hands of Time, The (Brian's Song)   *Listen Easy* (Philips 6308157); *Spotlight on Tony Bennett*, Vol. 1 (Philips 9299521)

Happiness Is a Thing Called Joe   *Tony Sings for Two* (BBL 7479)

Harlem Butterfly   *With Love* (CBS 84849)

Have I Told You Lately   *I Left My Heart in San Francisco* (CBS BPG 62201)

Have Yourself a Merry Little Christmas   *Snowfall: Tony Bennett Christmas Album* (CBS 637828)

Here   *Tony Sings the Great Hits of Today* (CBS 6392/89227)

Here, There and Everywhere   *Tony Sings the Great Hits of Today* (CBS 639628/81227)

Here's That Rainy Day   *With Love* (CBS 64849)

Hi-Ho   *Yesterday I Heard the Rain* (CBS 63351)

Home Is the Place   *Yesterday I Heard the Rain* (CBS 63351)

House Of The Flowers   *Tony Bennett Sings Harold Arlen* (BBL 7455, BBL 609); *Let's Fall in Love with the Songs of Harold Arlen* (CBS 80796)

How About You   *Tony Bennett at Carnegie Hall* (CBS BPG 62116)

How Beautiful Is The Night (With You)   *With Love* (CBS 64849)

How Can I Replace You?   *The Voice of Your Choice* (BBR 8051)

How Do You Say Auf Wiedersehn?   *For Once in my Life* (CBS BPG 63166)

How Insensitive   *If I Ruled the World – Songs for the Jet Set* (CBS BPG 62544); *Tony Bennett's Greatest Hits*, Vol. 2 (CBS 63612)

How Little We Know   *Listen Easy* (Philips 6308 157); *Spotlight on Tony Bennett*, Record 2 (Philips 9299 522); *At Long Last Love* (Philips SON 014)

How Long Has This Been Going On?   *Tony Bennett* (BBL 7452)

Hushabye Mountain *Yesterday I Heard the Rain* (CBS 63351)

I Am   *A String of Tony's Hits* (CBS DP 66010)

I Can't Believe that You're in Love with Me   *Cloud Seven* (BBR 8089)

I Can't Give You Anything But Love   *Tony Bennett Showcase* (BBL 7138)

I Concentrate on You   *Listen Easy* (Philips 6308 157); *Spotlight on Tony Bennett*, Record 2 (Philips 9299 522); *Words and Music* (Philips 9299 524); *At Long Last Love* (Philips SON 014)

I Cover the Waterfront   *Love Songs* (CBS 64444, 66297)

I Didn't Know What Time It Was   *Tony Sings for Two* (BBL 7479)

I Don't Know Why   *Tony Bennett Makes It Happen* (CBS BPG 63055)

I did not Know a Day I did not Love You (from the musical *Two by Two*) *Love Story* (CBS 64368)

I Fall in Love Too Easily   *Cloud Seven* (BBR 8089)

I Left My Heart in San Francisco   *Tony Bennett at Carnegie Hall* (CBS BPG 62116); *I Left My Heart in San Francisco* (CBS BPG 62201); *Tony's Greatest Hits* (BPG 62821); *Tony Bennett Sings His All-Time Hall of Fame Hits* (CBS 64200); *Get Happy in London with the London Philharmonic* (part of a medley) (CBS 64577); *Tony Bennett's All-Time Greatest Hits*, Record 2 (CBS 65283)

I Let a Song Go out of My Heart   *Tony Bennett Makes It Happen* (CBS BPG 63055)

I Love the Winter Weather   *Snowfall: The Tony Bennett Christmas Album* (CBS 637828)

I Only Have Eyes for You   *Yesterday I Heard the Rain* (CBS 63351); *Love Songs* (CBS 64443/66297)

I Walk a Little Faster   *Who Can I Turn To?* (CBS BPG 62486); *Let's Fall in Love with the Songs of Cy Coleman* (CBS 80797)

I Wanna Be Around   *I Wanna Be Around* (CBS BPG 62149); *Tony's Greatest Hits* (CBS BPG 62861); *Tony Bennett Sings His All-Time Hall of Fame Hits* (CBS 64200); *Get Happy with the London Philharmonic* (a medley) (CBS 64577); *Tony Bennett's All-Time Greatest Hits*, Record 2 (CBS 62583)

I Want To Be Happy   *Love Story* (CBS 64368); *Get Happy with the London Philharmonic* (CBS 64577)

I Will Live My Life for You   *I Wanna Be Around* (CBS BPG 62149)

If I Could Go Back   *Listen Easy* (Philips 6308157); *Spotlight on Tony Bennett*, Record 1 (Philips 9299 521); *At Long Last Love* (Philips SON 014)

If I Love Again   *I Wanna Be Around* (CBS BPG 62149)

If I Ruled the World   *If I Ruled the World – Songs for the Jet Set* (CBS BPG 62544); *Tony's Greatest Hits* (CBS BPG 62821); *Get Happy with the London Philharmonic* (CBS 64577)

If You Were Mine   *I Wanna Be Around* (CBS BPG 62149)

I'm Always Chasing Rainbows   *Tony Bennett* (BBL 7452); *I Left My Heart in San Francisco* (CBS BPG 62201)

I'll Be Around   *The Many Moods of Tony* (CBS BPG 62245)

I'll Be Seeing You   *Tony Bennett Showcase* (BBL 7138)

I'll Begin Again   *Love Story* (CBS 643681); *Get Happy with the London Philharmonic* (CBS 64577)

I'll Bring You a Rainbow   *A String of Tony's Hits*, Record 2 (CBS DB 66010)

I'll Only Miss Her When I Think of Her   *A Time for Love* (CBS BPG 62800)

I'm a Fool to Want You   *To My Wonderful One* (BBL 7413)

I'm Coming Home Virginia   *My Heart Sings* (BBL 7495)

I'm Just a Lucky So and So   *Tony Bennett Showcase* (BBL 7138); *Tony Bennett at Carnegie Hall* (CBS BPG 62116)

I'm Losing My Mind   *Summer of Fort-Two* (CBS 64848)

I'm Through with Love   *Tony Sings for Two* (BBL 7479); *Love Songs* (CBS 64444/66297)

In the Middle of an Island   *A String of Tony's Hits* (CBS DP 66010)

In the Wee Small Hours   *A Time for Love* (CBS BPG 62800)

Individual Things (from musical *Pretty Belle*)   *Love Story* (CBS 64368)

Invitation   *The Good Things in Life* (MGM 5088); Philips 6308134; *Spotlight on Tony Bennett*, Record 1 (Philips 9299521)

Irina my Inamorata   *Summer of Forty-Two* (CBS 64848)

Is That All There Is?   *Tony Sings the Great Hits of Today* (CBS 63962/81227)

It Amazes Me   *Long Ago and Far Away* (BBL 7280); *Tony Bennett at Carnegie Hall* (CBS BPG 62116); *Let's Fall in Love with the Songs of Cy Coleman* (CBS 80797)

It Could Happen to You   *Long Ago and Far Away* (BBL 7280); *When Lights Are Low* (CBS BPG 62296)

It Had To Be You   *Tony Bennett Showcase* (BBL 7138); *When Lights Are Low* (CBS BPG 62296); *Tony Bennett Sings His All-Time Hall of Fame Hits* (CBS 64200); *Love Songs* (CBS 64444/66297)

It Never Was You   *My Heart Sings* (BBL 7495)

It Was Me   *I Wanna Be Around* (CBS BPG 62149); *Summer of Forty-Two* (CBS 64848)

It Was You   *The Good Things in Life* (MGM 6088, Philips 6308134); *Spotlight On Tony Bennett*, Record 1 (Philips 9299521); *At Long Last Love* (Philips SON 014)

It Was Written in the Stars   *Tony Bennett Sings Harold Arlen* (BBL 7455, BBL 609); *Let's Fall in Love with the Songs of Harold Arlen* (CBS 80796)

It's a Sin To Tell a Lie *When Lights Are Low* (CBS BPG 62296)

It's Magic *Tony Bennett* (BBL 7452)

I've Got Just about Everything *When Lights Are Low* (CBS BPG 62296)

I've Got the World on a String *Tony Bennett Sings Harold Arlen* (BBL 7455, BBL 609); *Snowfall – The Tony Bennett Christmas Album* (63782); *Let's Fall In Love with the Songs of Harold Arlen* (CBS 80796)

I've Got Your Number *Let's Fall in Love with the Songs of Cy Coleman* (CBS 80797)

I've Never Seen *Who Can I Turn to?* (CBS BPG 62486)

Jingle Bells *Snowfall: The Tony Bennett Christmas Album* (CBS 63782)

Judy *When Lights Are Low* (CBS BPG 62296)

Just Friends *Tony Sings for Two* (BBL 7479)

Just in Time *In Person* (BBL 7308, CBS BPG 62250/32373); *Tony Bennett at Carnegie Hall* (CBS BPG 62116); *In Person (with Count Basie)* (CBS BPG 62250); *Tony Bennett's All-Time Greatest Hits* (CBS 65282); *A String of Tony's Hits*, Record 1 (66010)

Just One of Those Things *The Beauty of My Heart/Just One of Those Things* (BBL 7219, Harmony HS 11340)

Keep Smiling at Trouble *This Is All I Ask* (CBS BPG 62205); *For Once in My Life* (CBS BPG 63166)

Kid's a Dreamer, The *The Many Moods of Tony* (CBS BPG 62245)

Lady's in Love with You, The *Tony Bennett Makes It Happen* (CBS BPG 63055)

Last Night when We Were Young *To My Wonderful One* (BBL 7413)

Laura *To My Wonderful One* (BBL 7413); *I Only Have Eyes for You* (CBS 56444); *Love Songs* (CBS 66297)

Lazy Afternoon *The Beat of My Heart* (BBL 7219); *Just One of Those Things* (HS 11340); *Tony Bennett at Carnegie Hall*, Pt. 2 (CBS BPG 62117); *If I Ruled the World – Songs for the Jet Set* (CBS BPG 62544)

Lazy Days in Love *In Love* (CBS 64849)

Let There Be Love *The Beat of My Heart/Just One of Those Things* (BBL 7219, Harmony HS 11340); *Get Happy with the London Philharmonic* (CBS 64577)

181

Let's Begin *The Beat of My Heart* (Philips BBL 7219)

Let's Face the Music and Dance *The Beat of My Heart* (BBL 7219); *Just One of Those Things* (Harmony HS 11340)

Let's Fall in Love *Tony Bennett Sings Harold Arlen* (BBL 7455, BBL 609); *Let's Fall in Love with the Songs of Harold Arlen* (CBS 80796)

Limehouse Blues *The Many Moods of Tony* (CBS BPG 62245)

Listen, Little Girl *Who Can I Turn To?* (CBS BPG 862486)

Little Boy, The *The Many Moods of Tony* (CBS BPG 62245)

Little Green Apples *Tony Sings the Great Hits of Today* (CBS 63962/81227)

Living Together, Growing Together *At Long Last Love* (Philips SON 014)

London by Night *The Good Things in Life* (MGM 5088, Philips 6308134); *Spotlight on Tony Bennett*, Record 2 (9299522)

Lonely Place, A *I've Gotta Be Me* (CBS 636855)

Long and Winding Road, The *Tony Bennett's Something* (CBS 64217)

Look of Love, The *Tony Sings the Great Hits of Today* (CBS 63962/81227)

Lost in the Stars *Tony Bennett at Carnegie Hall*, Pt. 2 (CBS BPG 62117); *In Person (with Count Basie Orchestra)* (CBS BPG 62250)

Love *In Love* (CBS 64849)

Love for Sale *I Left my Heart in San Francisco* (CBS BPG 62201); *Love Songs* (CBS 64444, CBS 66297)

Love Is Here to Stay *Tony Bennett at Carnegie Hall* (CBS BPG 62116); *Yesterday I Heard the Rain* (CBS 63351)

Love Is the Thing *Listen Easy* (Philips 6308157); *Spotlight on Tony Bennett*, Record 1 (9299521)

Love Letters *Cloud Seven* (BBR 8089)

Love Look Away *Tony Bennett at Carnegie Hall*, Pt. 2 (CBS BPG 62117); *I Wanna Be Around* (CBS BPG 62149); *Tony Bennett's All-Time Greatest Hits* (CBS 65282); *A String of Tony's Hits* (CBS DP 66010)

Love Scene *If I Ruled the World – Songs for the Jet Set* (CBS BPG 62544)

Love Story (Where Do I Begin?) *Love Story* (CBS 64368); *Get Happy with the London Philharmonic* (CBS 64577); *Tony Bennett's All-Time Greatest Hits* (CBS 65282)

Lover Man   *My Heart Sings* (BBL 7495)

Long Ago and Far Away   *Long Ago and Far Away* (BBL 7280)

Look About Now   *This Is All I Ask* (CBS BPG 62205)

Lost in the Stars   *Tony Bennett Showcase* (BBL 7138); *In Person* (BBL 7308; CBS BPG 62250/32373)

Love for Sale *The Beat of My Heart/Just One of Those Things* (BBL 7219, Harmony HS 11340)

Love Walked In   *Tony Bennett Showcase* (BBL 7138)

Lullaby of Broadway   *In Person* (BBL 7308, BPG 62250/32373); *Tony Bennett at Carnegie Hall* (BPG 62116); *For Once in My Life* (CBS BPG 63166); *The Beat of My Heart/Just One of Those Things* (BBL 7219, Harmony HS 11340); *In Person (with Count Basie Orchestra)* (CBS BPG 62250)

Make it Easy on Yourself   *Tony Bennett's Something* (CBS 64217)

Mam'selle   *Tony Sings for Two* (BBL 7479)

Man that Got Away, The   *Tony Sings for Two* (BBL 7479)

Marry Young   *I Left My Heart in San Francisco* (CBS BPG 62201)

Maybe September   *The Movie Song Album* (CBS BPG 62677)

Maybe This Time   *Tony Bennett's All-Time Greatest Hits* (CBS 65282)

MacArthur Park   *Tony Sings the Great Hits of Today* (CBS 639628/81227)

Midnight Sun, The   *At Long Last Love* (Philips SON 014); *The Good Things in Life* (MGM 5088, Philips 6308134); *Spotlight on Tony Bennett*, Vol. 1 (Philips 9299521)

Mimi   *The Good Things in Life* (MGM 5088, Philips 6308134); *A Touch of Class* (Philips 64999 931); *Spotlight on Tony Bennett*, Vol. 2 (Philips 9299 522)

Moment of Truth, The   *This Is All I Ask* (CBS BPG 62205); *Tony's Greatest Hits* (BPG 62821)

More and More   *Summer of Forty-Two* (CBS 64848)

More Than You Know   *My Heart Sings* (BBL 7495)

My Baby Just Cares for Me   *Cloud Seven* (BBR 8089)

My Cherie Amour   *Tony Sings the Great Hits of Today* (CBS 63962/81227)

My Favourite Things   *Tony Bennett's Greatest Hits*, Vol. 2 (CBS 631612); *Snowfall – The Tony Bennett Christmas Album* (CBS 637825)

My Foolish Heart   *Long Ago and Far Away* (BBL 7280)

My Funny Valentine *Tony Sings for Two* (BBL 7499); *A Time for Love* (CBS BPG 62800); *Love Songs* (CBS 64444/66297); *Listen Easy* (Philips 6308 157); *A Touch of Class* (Philips 6499 932); *Spotlight on Tony Bennett*, Record 2 (9299 522)

My Heart Sings *My Heart Sings* (BBL 7495)

My Heart Tells Me *Cloud Seven* (BBR 8089); *Tony Bennett at Carnegie Hall*, Pt. 2 (CBS BPG 62117)

My Love *Spotlight on Tony Bennett*, Record 2 (Philips 9299 522); *At Long Last Love* (Philips SON 014)

My Ship *My Heart Sings* (Philips BBL 7495); *If I Ruled the World – Songs For the Jet Set* (CBS BPG 62544)

Never Too Late *The Movie Song Album* (CBS BPG 62677)

Nobody Else but Me *When Lights Are Low* (CBS BPG 62296)

Nobody's Heart Belonged to Me *Tony Sings for Two* (BBL 7479)

O Sole Mio *Spotlight on Tony Bennett*, Record 1 (Philips 9299521); *At Long Last Love* (Philips SON 014)

Oh, Lady Be Good *The Good Things in Life* (MGM 5088, Philips 6308134); *Spotlight on Tony Bennett*, Record 2 (Philips 9299522)

Oh! You Crazy Moon *When Lights are Low* (CBS BPG 62296)

Ol' Man River *In Person* (BBL 7308, CBS BPG 62250/32373); *Tony Bennett at Carnegie Hall* (CBS BPG 62116)

Old Devil Moon *Cloud Seven* (BBR 8089); *Tony Bennett Makes It Happen* (CBS BPG 63055); *Get Happy with the London Philharmonic* (CBS 64577)

On a Clear Day You Can See Forever *Tony Bennett's Something* (64217)

On Green Dolphin Street *When Lights Are Low* (CBS BPG 62296)

On the Other Side Of the Tracks *This Is All I Ask* (CBS BPG 62205); *Let's Fall in Love with the Songs of Cy Coleman* (CBS 80797)

On the Sunny Side of the Street *Tony Bennett Makes It Happen* (CBS BPG 63055); *Get Happy with the London Philharmonic* (CBS 64577); *Listen Easy* (Philips 6308 157); *Spotlight on Tony Bennett*, Record 1 (929952)

Once in a Garden (The Garden of the Finzi-Continis) *Listen Easy* (Philips 6308 157); *Spotlight on Tony Bennett*, Record 1 (Philips 9299 521)

Once upon a Summertime *I Wanna Be Around* (CBS BPG 62149); *Tony's Greatest Hits* (CBS BPG 62821)

Once Upon a Time   *I Left My Heart in San Francisco* (CBS BPG 62201); *Tony's Greatest Hits* (CBS BPG 62821)

One for my Baby   *Tony Bennett at Carnegie Hall*, Pt 2 (CBS BPG 62117); *Tony Bennett Sings His All-Time Hall of Fame Hits* (CBS 64200)

Only the Young   *Yesterday I Heard the Rain* (CBS 63351)

O Sole Mio   *The Good Things in Life* (MGM 5088, Phillips 6308134)

Out of This World   *Tony Bennett* (BBL 7452); *For Once in My Life* (CBS BPG 63166)

Over the Rainbow   *Tony Bennett Sings Harold Arlen* (BBL 7455, BBL 609); *Let's Fall in Love with the Songs of Harold Arlen* (CBS 80796)

Over the Sun   *I've Gotta Be Me* (CBS 63685)

Passing Strangers   MGM 5088, Philips 6308 134; *At Long Last Love* (Philips SON 014)

Pawnbroker, The   *The Movie Song Album* CBS BPG 62677)

Pennies from Heaven   *In Person* (BBL 7308, GBS BPG 62250/ 32373); *In Person (with Count Basie)* (CBS BPG 62250)

Penthouse Serenade   *Love Songs* (CBS 66297)

Play It Again, Sam   *I've Gotta Be Me* (CBS 63685)

People   *Tony Bennett's Greatest Hits*, Vol. 2 (CBS 63612)

Poor Butterfly   *Tony Bennett* (BBL 7452)

Put on a Happy Face   *Tony Bennett's All-Time Greatest Hits* (CBS 65282); *A String of Tony's Hits*, Record 2 (CBS DP 66010)

Quiet Nights   *I Wanna Be Around* (CBS BPG 62149)

Rags to Riches   *Tony Bennett at Carnegie Hall*, Pt 2 (CBS BPG 62117); *Tony Bennett Sings His All-Time Hall of Fame Hits* (CBS 64200); *Tony Bennett's All-Time Greatest Hits* (CBS 65282)

Rain Rain (Don't Go Away)   *Listen Easy* (Philips 6308 157); *Spotlight on Tony Bennett*, Vol. 2 (Philips 9299 522)

Remind Me   *With Love* (CBS 64849)

Right as Rain   *Tony Bennett Sings Harold Arlen* (BBL 7455, BBL 609); *Let's Fall in Love with the Songs of Harold Arlen* (CBS 80796)

Right to Love, The   *If I Ruled the World – Songs for the Jet Set* (CBS BPG 62544)

Riviera, The   *In Love* (CBS 64849); *Let's Fall in Love in the Songs of Cy Coleman* (CBS 80797)

Rules of the Road, The   *I Left My Heart in San Francisco* (CBS

BPG 6220); *When Lights Are Low* (CBS BPG 62296); *Lets Fall in Love in the Songs of Cy Coleman* (CBS 80797)

Samba de Orfeu *The Movie Song Album* (CBS BPG 62677)

Santa Claus Is Comin' to Town *Snowfall – The Tony Bennett Christmas Album* (CBS 63782)

Se te Olvida *Tony Bennett's Something* (CBS 64217)

Second Time Around, The *Love Songs* (CBS 66297, CBS 64444 (2 vols)); *The Move Song Album* (CBS BPG 62677)

September One *To My Wonderful One* (BBL 7413)

September Song *Love Songs* (CBS 64444/66297)

Sandy's Smile *This Is All I Ask* (CBS BPG 62205)

Shadow of Your Smile, The *Tony Bennett's Greatest Hits*, Vol. 2 (CBS 63612); *The Movie Song Album* (CBS BPG 62677); *Tony Bennett Sings His All-Time Hall of Fame Hits* (CBS 64200); *Tony Bennett's All-Time Greatest Hits* (CBS 65282)

She's Funny That Way *Tony Bennett Makes It Happen* (CBS BPG 63055)

Shining Sea, The *A Time for Love* (CBS BPG 62800); *Summer of Forty-Two* (CBS 64848)

Silent Night Holy Night *Snowfall – The Tony Bennett Christmas Album* (CBS 63782)

Sing You Sinners *Back at Carnegie Hall* (CBS BPG 62117); *Tony's All-Time Greatest Hits*, Record 2 (CBS 65283); *A String of Tony's Hits*, Record 1 (CBS DP 66010)

Sleepin' Me, A *Tony Sings Songs for Two* (BBL 7479)

Sleepy Time *A Time for Two* (CBS BPG 62800)

Smile *I Left My Heart in San Francisco* (CBS BPG 62201); *The Movie Song Album* (CBS BPG 62677); *Tony's All-Time Greatest Hits*, Record 2 (CBS 65283); *A String of Tony's Hits*, Record 2 (CBS DP 66010)

So Beats My Heart for You *The Beat of My Heart* (BBL 7219)

So Far *Long Ago and Far Away* (BBL 7280)

So Long, Big Time! *The Many Moods of Tony* (CBS BPG 62245)

Solitaire *The Last Picture Show* (CBS 70115)

Solitude *In Person* (BBL 7308, CBS BPG 62250/323734); *Tony Bennett at Carnegie Hall* (CBS BPG 62116); *In Person (with Count Basie)* (CBS BPG 62250)

Some of These Days *Spotlight on Tony Bennett*, Record 1 (9299521)

Someone to Light up My Life *The Good Things in Life* (MGM)

5088, Philips 6308134); *Spotlight on Tony Bennett*, Record 1 (9299 521); *At Long Last Love* (Philips SON 014)

Someone to Love   *I Wanna Be Around* (CBS BPG 62149)

Something   *Tony Sings the Greatest Hits of Today* (CBS 63962/81227); *Tony Bennett Sings Something* (CBS 64217); *Tony Bennett's All-Time Greatest Hits* (CBS 65282)

Something's Gotta Give   *The Voice of Your Choice* (BBR 8051)

Sometimes I'm Happy   *Tony Bennett at Carnegie Hall*, Pt 2 (CBS BPG 62117); *For Once in My Life* (CBS BPG 63166)

Something in Your Smile   *For Once in My Life* (BPG 63166)

Somewhere Along the Line   *Summer of Forty-Two* (CBS 64848)

Song of the Jet   *If I Ruled the World – Songs for the Jet Set* (CBS BPG 62544)

Soon It's Gonna Rain   *The Many Words of Tony* (CBS BPG 62245); *Love Story* (CBS 64368)

Sophisticated Lady   *Tony Bennett* (BBL 7452)

Speak Low   *When Lights Are Low* (CBS BPG 62296); *To My Wonderful One* (BBL 7413)

Spring in Manhattan   *The Many Moods of Tony* (CBS BPG 62245)

Stella by Starlight   *My Heart Sings* (BBL 7495); *Love Songs* (CBS 64443)

Streets of Dreams   *Tony Sings for Two* (BBL 7419); *Love Songs* (CBS 64443)

Stranger in Paradise   *The Voice of Your Choice* (BBR 5051); *Tony Bennett at Carnegie Hall* (CBS BPG 62116); *Tony Bennett's All-Time Greatest Hits* (CBS 65283); *A String of Tony's Hits*, Record 1 (CBS DP 66010)

Suddenly   *To My Wonderful One* (BBL 7413)

Summer Knows, The   *Summer of Forty-Two* (CBS BPG 64848)

Sunrise Sunset   *Tony Sings the Great Hits of Today* (CBS 6392/81227)

Sweet Georgie Fame   *Yesterday I Heard the Rain* (CBS 63351)

Sweet Lorraine   *If I Ruled the World – Songs for the Jet Set* (CBS BPG 62544)

Take Me Back Again   *The Voice of Your Choice* (BBR 8051)

Takin' a Chance on Love   *Tony Bennett Showcase* (BBL 7138); *In Person* (BBL 7308/CBS BPG 62250/32373); *I Left My Heart in San Francisco* (CBS BPG 62201)

Taste of Honey, A   *The Many Moods of Tony* (CBS BPG 62245); *Tony's Greatest Hits* (CBS BPG 62821); *Love Story* (CBS 643685); *CBS Showcase*, Record 2 (CBS 66205B)

Tea for Two   *Love Story* (CBS 64368); *Get Happy with the London Philharmonic* (CBS 64577)

Tell Her That It's Snowing   *Listen Easy* (Philips 6308 157); *Spotlight on Tony Bennett*, Record 2 (PL 9299 522)

Tell Me that You Love Me   *The Voice of Your Choice* (BBR 8051)

Tender Is the Night   *I Left My Heart in San Francisco* (CBS BPG 62201); *Love Songs* (CBS 64443)

Tenderly   *To My Wonderful One* (BBL 7413); *Love Songs* (CBS 64444/66297)

That Night   *I've Gotta Be Me* (CBS 636685)

Then Was Then and Now Is Now   *If I Ruled the World – Songs for the Jet Set* (CBS BPG 62544); *Let's Fall in Love with the Songs of Cy Coleman* (CBS 80797)

There Will Never Be Another You   *In Person* (BBL 7308); CBS BPG (622505/32373); *In Person (with Count Basie)* (CBS BPG 62250); *Yesterday I Heard the Rain* (CBS BPG 63351); *Get Happy with the London Philharmonic* (CBS 64577)

There'll Be No Teardrops Tonight   *The Voice of Your Choice* (BBR 8051); *A String of Tony's Hits*, Record 1 (CBS DP 66010)

There's a Lull in My Life   *Who Can I Turn To* (CBS BPG 62486)

These Foolish Things   *Tony Bennett Showcase* (BBL 7138)

They All Laughed   *I've Gotta Be Me* (CBS 63668)

They Can't Take That Away from Me   *For Once in My Life* (CBS BPG 63166); *Love Story* (CBS 64368)

Think How It's Gonna Be (from the musical *Applause*) *Tony Bennett's Something* (CBS 64217)

This Is All I Ask   *This Is All I Ask* (CBS BPG 62205); *Tony's Greatest Hits* (BPG 62821); *Tony Bennett Sings His All-Time Hall of Fame Hits* (CBS 64200)

This Is All I Ask   *Tony Bennett* (BBL 7452); *This Is All I Ask* (CBS BPG 62205); *Tony Bennett's All-Time Greatest Hits*, Record 2 (65283)

This Time the Dream's On Me   *Tony Bennett Sings Harold Arlen* (BBL 7455, BBL 609); *Let's Fall in Love with the Songs of Harold Arlen* (CBS 80796)

Till   *To My Wonderful One* (BBL 7413); *Love Songs* (CBS 64444); *Summer of Forty-Two* (CBS 64848); *Love Songs* (CBS 66297)

Time after Time   *Long Ago and Far Away* (BBL 7280)

Time for Love, A   *A Time for Love* (CBS BPG 62800); *Tony Bennett's Greatest Hits*, vol. 2 (CBS 63612); *Tony Bennett's All-Time Greatest Hits*, Record 2 (CBS 65283)

Toot, Toot, Tootsie   *My Heart Sings* (BBL 7495)

Touch the Earth   *A Time for Love* (CBS BPG 62800)

Trapped in the Web of Love   *A Time for Love* (CBS BPG 62800)

Trolley Song, The   *The Movie Song Album* (CBS BPG 62677); *Get Happy with the London Philharmonic* (CBS BPG 64577)

True Blue Lou   *This Is All I Ask* (CBS BPG 62205)

Twilight World   *With Love* (CBS 64849)

Until I Met You   *I Wanna Be Around* (CBS BPG 62149)

Valley of the Dolls   *I've Gotta Be One* (CBS 63685)

Very Thought of You, The   *A Time for Love* (CBS BPG 62800); *Love Songs* (CBS 6443/66297)

Vivre pour Vivre (Live for Life)   *Tony Sings the Great Hits Of Today* (CBS 63962/81227)

Walkabout   *Summer of Forty-Two* (CBS 64848)

Walk in the Country   *Tony Bennett* (BBL 7452)

Waltz for Debbie   *Who Can I Turn To?* (CBS BPG 62486)

Watch What Happens   *If I Ruled the World – Songs for the Jet Set* (CBS BPG 62544); *Tony Bennett's Greatest Hits*, Vol. 2 (63612)

Wave   *Tony Bennett's Something* (CBS 64217); *Get Happy with the London Philharmonic* (CBS 64577)

Way I Feel, The   *This Is All I Ask* (CBS BPG 62205)

Way You Look Tonight, The   *Long Ago and Far Away* (BBL 7280)

We Mustn't Say Goodbye   *To My Wonderful One* (BBL 7413)

We Wish You a Merry Christmas   *Snowfall – The Tony Bennett Christmas Album* (CBS 63782)

What a Wonderful World   *Tony Bennett's Something* (CBS 64217)

What Good Does It Do   *Tony Bennett at Carnegie Hall*, Pt 2 (CBS BPG 62117); *Tony Bennett Sings Harold Arlen* (BBL 7455, BBL 609)

What Makes It Happen?   *Tony Bennett Makes It Happen* (CBS BPG 63055)

What the World Needs Now Is Love   *I've Gotta Be Me* (CBS 63685); *Get Happy with the London Philharmonic* (CBS 64577)

What Will I Tell My Heart? *The Voice of your Choice* (BBR 8051)

When I Fall in Love *In Person* (BBL 7308, CBS BPG 62250/ 32373); *In Person (with Count Basie)* (CBS BPG 62250)

When I Look in Your Eyes (from the film *Doctor Dolittle*) *Tony Bennett's Something* (CBS 64217)

When Joanna Loved Me *The Many Moods of Tony* (CBS BPG 62245); *Tony's Greatest Hits* (CBS 62821); *Love Story* (CBS 64368)

When Lights Are Low (CBS BPG 62296)

When the Sun Comes Out *Tony Bennett Sings Harold Arlen* (BBL 7455, BBL 609); *Let's Fall in Love with the Songs of Harold Arlen* (CBS 80796)

When We're Alone Love Songs (CBS 64443)

Where Is Love? (with choir) *Snowfall – The Tony Bennett Christmas Album* (CBS 63782)

Where or When *Tony Sings for Two* (BBL 7479); Love Songs (CBS 64443, 66297)

While the Music Plays On *Cloud Seven* (BBR 8089)

White Christmas *Snowfall – The Tony Bennett Christmas Album* (CBS 63782)

Without a Song *Tony Bennett Showcase* (BBL 7138); *In Person* (BBL 7308, CBS BPG 62250/32373)

Who Can I Turn To? *Who Can I Turn To?* (CBS BPG 62486); *Tony's Greatest Hits* (BPG 62821); *Tony Bennett Sings His All-Time Hall of Fame Hits* (CBS 64200); *Tony Bennett's All-Time Greatest Hits*, Record 2 (CBS 65283)

Whoever You Are I Love You *I've Gotta Be Me* (CBS 63685)

Winter Wonderland *Snowfall – Tony Bennett's Christmas Album* (PB 63782)

Wonderful One *To My Wonderful One* (BBL 7413)

Wrap Your Troubles in Dreams *Who Can I Turn To?* (CBS BPG 62486)

Yesterdays *In Time for Love* (CBS BPG 62800)

Yesterday I Heard the Rain *Yesterday I Heard the Rain* (CBS 63351); *Tony Bennett's Greatest Hits*, Vol. 2 (CBS 63612); *Tony Sings His All-Time Hall of Fame Hits* (CBS 64200)

You Can Depend on Me *Tony Bennett Showcase* (BBL 7138)

You Can't Love 'em All *A String of Tony's Hits*, Record 2 (CBS DP 66010)

You Took Advantage of Me   *My Heart Sings* (BBL 7495)

You'll Never Get away from Me   *A String of Tony's Hits*, Record 2 (CBS DP 66010)

Young and Foolish   *This Is All I Ask* (CBS BPG 62205)

Young Warm And Wonderful   *A String of Tony's Hits*, Record 2 (CBS DP 66010)

You've Changed   *The Many Moods of Tony*   (CBS BPG 62245)